INCREASINGLY LOCAL
How AI Transforms Local Busin‹

MW01601165

Client Privacy and Case Study Disclosure

The case studies, examples, and client stories featured throughout this book are based on real businesses and actual results achieved through the implementation of the strategies described. However, to protect client privacy and maintain confidentiality, the following measures have been taken:

- Names have been changed: All personal names, business names, and specific company identifiers have been modified or anonymized
- Locations have been generalized: Specific cities, neighborhoods, and geographic references have been altered or made generic while maintaining regional relevance
- Industry details may be modified: Some business type specifications have been adjusted to prevent identification while preserving the integrity of the strategic lessons
- Results are accurate: All performance metrics, growth percentages, and outcome data represent actual client achievements, though they may be rounded for clarity

These modifications ensure client confidentiality while allowing readers to learn from real-world implementations of AI-powered local marketing strategies. Any resemblance to actual businesses or individuals with the names used is purely coincidental.

Professional Advice Disclaimer

The strategies and recommendations in this book are based on the author's professional experience and documented client results. However, individual business circumstances vary, and results cannot be guaranteed. Readers should adapt strategies to their specific business situations and local markets, consult with qualified professionals for legal, financial, or technical implementation questions, and conduct their own due diligence when selecting AI tools or service providers.

The author and publisher make no warranties or guarantees regarding the effectiveness of these strategies for any particular business or situation.

DEDICATION

To the local business owners who serve their communities with passion and dedication, may AI amplify your impact while preserving what makes you irreplaceable.

TABLE OF CONTENTS

ACKNOWLEDGMENTS

This book exists because of the incredible people who believed in both the vision and the journey to get here.

First and foremost, to my wife, you've been my constant through every entrepreneurial adventure, late-night strategy session, and ambitious project that seemed impossible until it wasn't. Your unwavering support gave me the confidence to help other business owners transform their companies, and your patience during the countless hours spent working through the lessons that made this book possible. Thank you for believing in what we're building together.

To my clients, you are the real authors of this book. Every strategy, every insight, and every case study come from your willingness to trust me with your businesses and try new approaches. You didn't just hire a marketing consultant; you became partners in proving that local businesses can compete and win in an AI-driven world. Your courage to implement these strategies, your feedback that made them better, and your success that validated the approach are what make this book valuable. Thank you for letting me be part of your growth stories.

To every local business owner who has ever felt overwhelmed by digital marketing or frustrated by competitors who seem to have advantages you don't, this book is my commitment to changing that. You have more capability and opportunity than you realize.

The journey from idea to implementation is never solo. This book represents the collective wisdom and courage of everyone who chooses to build something meaningful in their community.

Thank you for being part of that journey.

Phil Tucker
August 2025

LOCAL BUSINESS MEETS AI: YOUR COMPETITIVE EDGE

Here's what I learned after helping 300+ local businesses transform their digital presence: the ones that survive and thrive aren't necessarily the biggest or the oldest. They're the ones that adapt fastest.

I started Be Famous Media in 2012 with a simple mission, help local service businesses turn their websites into lead-generation machines. Back then, it was all about getting the basics right: clean website design, solid SEO fundamentals, and some pay-per-click advertising. The formula worked. Local businesses saw more calls, more customers, more revenue.

But something shifted around 2023. The businesses that were just "doing SEO" started falling behind. Meanwhile, the ones that embraced AI-powered marketing strategies began dominating their local markets in ways I'd never seen before.

Let me tell you about Sarah, who owns a physical therapy practice. When we first started working together, she was getting maybe 10-15 new patient inquiries per month through her website. Good, but not great. Then we implemented what you'll learn in this book, AI-powered local marketing strategies that most of her competitors didn't even know existed.

Within six months, Sarah was fielding 40+ qualified inquiries monthly. Her Google Business Profile became the most engaging in her area. Her website started ranking for dozens of local search terms she never thought to target. Most importantly, her practice grew from 2 therapists to 6, and she opened a second location.

What changed? Sarah didn't just adopt AI tools, she integrated them strategically into every aspect of her local marketing. She used AI to understand exactly what her potential patients were searching for, created content that answered their specific questions, optimized her online presence for voice search, and automated the processes that used to eat up hours of her time.

The result wasn't just more leads. It was the right leads, at the right time, with the right message.

That's what this book is about. Not the latest AI gimmick or some theoretical marketing strategy. This is about practical, tested approaches that local businesses can implement starting today to gain a serious competitive advantage.

Why AI Changes Everything for Local Business

Here's the reality: your customers aren't searching the way they did five years ago. They're asking Siri where to find the best pizza nearby. They're using Google Lens to identify that weird noise their car is making. They're expecting instant, personalized answers to hyperlocal questions.

Your competitors who understand this are capturing those customers. The ones who don't are watching their market share disappear.

AI levels the playing field in ways that weren't possible before. A single-location restaurant can now create personalized content for dozens of neighborhood-specific search terms. A three-person accounting firm can automate review management that used to require a full-time marketing coordinator. A home services contractor can optimize their online presence 24/7 without hiring an agency.

But here's what most business owners get wrong about AI: they think it's about replacing human connection with robots. That's backwards.

The best AI implementations amplify human connection. They help you be more personal, more responsive, and more relevant to your local customers, not less.

The Five Big Ideas That Will Transform Your Local Business

As you read this book, keep these core principles in mind:

1. AI isn't a luxury, it's a necessity for local businesses today

While you're debating whether to embrace AI, your competitors are using it to understand customer behavior, create better content, and capture more market share. The question isn't whether you should use AI. It's whether you want to lead or follow in your local market.

2. Smart automation helps small businesses with limited resources compete with anyone

You don't need a marketing team of 20 people to dominate local search. You need the right AI tools applied strategically. I'll show you how a solo practitioner can have the online presence of a multi-location business.

3. AI personalizes your marketing at scale, without losing the local touch

This is where most businesses mess up. They think AI means generic, robotic content. Done right, AI helps you create more personalized, locally relevant experiences than you could ever manage manually.

4. Data-driven insights turn local search visibility into measurable growth

AI doesn't just help you rank better, it helps you understand exactly which marketing activities drive real business results. You'll stop guessing about what works and start knowing.

5. AI tools must be woven into a complete strategy for real impact

Random AI experiments won't transform your business. But AI integrated into a comprehensive local marketing strategy? That's where the magic happens.

Your AI-Powered Local Marketing Transformation

Throughout this book, I'll share the specific strategies, tools, and processes that transformed businesses like Sarah's. You'll learn:

- How to use AI to audit your local online presence and identify quick wins
- The AI-powered keyword research that reveals exactly what your customers are searching for
- Content creation strategies that produce locally relevant material in minutes, not hours
- Google Business Profile optimization that makes you impossible to ignore
- Review management systems that build trust and credibility automatically
- Local link building that happens while you sleep
- Voice search optimization that captures the growing mobile audience
- Analytics that show you exactly where to focus your efforts for maximum impact

More importantly, you'll learn how to implement these strategies without getting overwhelmed by technology or losing the personal touch that makes local businesses special.

What Makes This Different

I'm not going to promise you'll dominate Google in 30 days or triple your revenue overnight. What I will show you is a systematic approach to using AI that builds sustainable competitive advantages over time.

Every strategy in this book has been tested with real businesses in real markets. The case studies you'll read aren't theoretical, they're from actual clients who implemented these methods and saw measurable results.

I'll also be completely transparent about what works, what doesn't, and when to use human judgment instead of automation. AI is powerful, but it's not magic. Success comes from applying it strategically, not randomly.

Who This Book Is For

You might be a restaurant owner tired of seeing competitors show up first in local searches. Maybe you're a professional services provider who knows your expertise is better than the guy ranking above you. Perhaps you run a home services business and want to capture more of those "emergency" searches that turn into high-value customers.

Whatever your business, if you serve customers in a specific geographic area and want to use AI to grow smarter instead of harder, this book is for you.

You don't need to be tech-savvy to implement these strategies. You just need to be willing to try new approaches and commit to consistent execution.

A Personal Note

I've watched AI transform how local businesses connect with their customers. The businesses that embrace these changes thoughtfully are thriving. The ones that ignore them are struggling to stay relevant.

My goal isn't just to teach you AI tactics. It's to help you build a local business that customers choose first, competitors respect, and you're proud to own.

The strategies in this book work because they're built on a simple truth: AI should make your business more human, not less. It should help you serve your local community better, not replace the relationships that make local business special.

Ready to get started? Let's transform your local business with AI that actually works.

Key Insights

"AI shouldn't distract local businesses, it should multiply their reach."
"Visibility without context is just noise, AI gives your business context."
"You can't scale trust, but you can automate the signals that build it."
"People don't search, they ask. AI helps you answer."
"Local means personal. AI helps you do that personally, at scale."

MAPPING YOUR LOCAL DIGITAL TERRITORY WITH AI

Mike thought his plumbing business was doing fine online. His website looked professional, he had a Google Business Profile, and he occasionally got calls from online searches. But when I asked him to walk me through his actual digital presence, the conversation got interesting fast.

"How many places can customers find you online?" I asked.
"Well, there's my website, Google, and I think we're on Yelp..."
"What about the 47 other directories where your business information appears?"
Mike's face went blank. "Forty-seven?"

That's when I showed him what an AI-powered audit revealed about his digital footprint. His business name was listed differently across 23 directories. His phone number had three variations. His address showed up as both "Street" and "St." in different places. His website took 8.2 seconds to load on mobile, an eternity in local search.

Most damaging of all, there were two duplicate Google Business Profiles for his company, splitting his reviews and confusing potential customers about which location was real.

Within three hours, AI tools had identified 31 specific issues that were quietly undermining his local search presence. Issues that would have taken weeks to find manually, if we'd found them at all.

Six weeks after fixing these problems, Mike's local search visibility increased 340%. His phone started ringing so much he hired another plumber.

This is what AI auditing can do for local businesses. Not in theory, in practice, with measurable results.

Why Traditional Audits Miss the Mark

Here's what most local business audits look like: someone checks if your website works, glances at your Google Business Profile, maybe runs your site through a speed test, and calls it good.

That approach misses 80% of what actually affects your local search performance.

Modern local SEO happens across dozens of platforms, hundreds of data points, and thousands of potential search queries. Your visibility depends on:
- Consistency across 50+ online directories
- Mobile performance under real network conditions
- Voice search optimization for conversational queries
- Review sentiment patterns across multiple platforms
- Local search ranking factors that change monthly
- Competitor movements in your specific market
- User behavior signals Google tracks but doesn't publicize

No human can efficiently audit all of these factors. But AI can analyze everything in hours, not weeks.

The Five Pillars of AI-Powered Local Audits

1. AI Speed Reveals What Manual Audits Miss

When I audit a local business manually, I might check 20-30 directories for consistent business information. An AI tool checks 200+ in minutes, identifying discrepancies that would never show up on my radar.

The same applies to technical issues. AI crawlers test your website performance from dozens of locations, on multiple device types, under various network conditions. They spot mobile usability problems that only affect certain phone models, page speed issues that only occur during peak traffic times, and broken functionality that works fine in your office but fails for customers.

A restaurant owner recently asked me why their online orders dropped every Friday night. Manual testing showed nothing wrong. AI analysis revealed their order form timing out under heavy load, only during peak hours when they needed it most. One server configuration fix brought Friday orders back to normal levels.

2. Pattern Detection in Reviews, Rankings, and Listings

AI excels at finding patterns humans miss. It can analyze 500 customer reviews and identify that 73% of negative feedback mentions "parking" while 89% of positive reviews highlight "staff friendliness." That's actionable intelligence for improving both your service and your marketing message.

The same pattern recognition applies to your search rankings. AI tracking shows you're ranking well for "emergency plumber" but poorly for "drain cleaning", even though you offer both services equally. That insight drives your content and optimization priorities.

Or consider business listing inconsistencies. AI might discover that every directory listing your business phone number as "(555) 123-4567" gets higher engagement than listings using "555.123.4567" format. Small detail, big impact on local search performance.

3. Competitive Intelligence That Actually Helps

Most competitive analysis looks at obvious metrics: who ranks higher, who has more reviews. AI-powered audits dig deeper.

They reveal that your main competitor gets 40% of their local traffic from a neighborhood blog you didn't know existed. They show that competing businesses are ranking for 23 local keywords you're not targeting but should be. They identify content gaps where customers are searching but no local business is providing good answers.

I worked with a home services contractor who was losing business to a competitor despite having better reviews and more experience. AI analysis showed the competitor

6

was optimized for voice search queries like "who fixes water heaters today" while my client was only optimized for text searches like "water heater repair." One content update later, the voice search traffic started flowing his way.

4. Prioritizing Actionable Insights Over Endless Reports

The biggest problem with most audits isn't missing information, it's having too much information without knowing what matters most.

AI auditing tools don't just identify problems. They prioritize fixes based on potential impact, difficulty of implementation, and current performance gaps. Instead of a 47-page report listing everything wrong, you get a ranked action plan starting with the highest-impact improvements.

For example, AI might identify that fixing your Google Business Profile's category selection will impact rankings more than updating 15 minor directory listings. Or that improving your mobile page speed will drive more calls than optimizing for three additional keywords. You focus on what moves the needle, not busy work.

5. Quick-Win Content and Optimization Tasks

The best AI audits don't just find problems, they suggest solutions.

When AI analysis reveals you're missing traffic for "same-day service" searches in your area, it can also suggest content topics, page structures, and even draft headlines that target those searches effectively.

If the audit shows customers frequently ask about pricing in reviews, AI can generate FAQ content addressing those concerns before they become negative reviews.

When technical issues are identified, AI tools INCREASINGLY ly provide step-by-step fixes or even automatically resolve simple problems like image compression and basic mobile optimization.

The AI Audit Process That Gets Results

Here's how I run AI-powered local audits for maximum impact:

Phase 1: Digital Footprint Mapping (30 minutes)

AI tools crawl the web to find every mention of your business across directories, review sites, social platforms, and local websites. This creates a complete map of your digital presence, often revealing listings you forgot existed.

The analysis identifies:
- Business information inconsistencies across platforms
- Duplicate or conflicting listings
- Unclaimed profiles where you're missing opportunities
- Directories where competitors are listed but you're not

Phase 2: Technical Performance Analysis (45 minutes)

AI crawlers test your website's performance from multiple locations and devices, simulating real customer experiences. They identify:

- Mobile usability issues that affect local search rankings
- Page speed problems that cause customers to leave
- Technical SEO issues that prevent proper indexing
- Local schema markup opportunities
- Contact form functionality across different scenarios

Phase 3: Local Search Visibility Assessment (60 minutes)

AI tools check your rankings for hundreds of local keyword combinations, including:

- Traditional text searches customers type
- Voice search queries they speak
- Seasonal and trending local terms
- Competitor comparison for market share analysis
- Maps visibility across different neighborhoods in your service area

Phase 4: Review and Reputation Analysis (30 minutes)

AI sentiment analysis processes all your online reviews to identify:
- Common themes in positive and negative feedback
- Specific service or product mentions that drive satisfaction
- Operational issues customers mention repeatedly
- Opportunities to highlight strengths in marketing
- Response strategy recommendations for negative reviews

Phase 5: Competitive Gap Analysis (45 minutes)

AI comparison tools analyze how you stack up against local competitors:
- Keywords they rank for that you don't
- Content topics they cover that you're missing
- Local directories where they have stronger presence
- Review acquisition strategies that work in your market
- Social media tactics driving engagement in your industry

Turning Audit Data Into Action

The goal isn't just to identify problems, it's to fix them in order of impact. Here's how to prioritize your AI audit findings:

Immediate Fixes (Week 1)
- Claim unclaimed business listings
- Fix critical business information inconsistencies
- Resolve technical issues preventing mobile access
- Update Google Business Profile with missing information

Quick Wins (Weeks 2-4)
- Optimize for high-traffic keywords you're close to ranking for
- Create content addressing common customer questions from reviews
- Improve page speed and mobile experience
- Set up automated review request systems

Long-term Strategy (Months 2-3)
- Develop content plans targeting competitive keyword gaps
- Build relationships with local directories and websites for link building
- Implement voice search optimization across all content
- Create systematic processes for maintaining listing consistency

Common AI Audit Discoveries

After running hundreds of these audits, certain patterns emerge:

The "Invisible Business" Problem: 67% of local businesses have significant presence gaps, they're simply not listed where customers expect to find them.

The "Consistency Crisis": 89% have business information variations that confuse both customers and search engines.

The "Mobile Disaster": 43% have websites that technically work on mobile but provide poor user experiences that drive customers away.

The "Voice Search Gap": 78% aren't optimized for how people actually speak their searches, missing growing mobile traffic.

The "Review Response Failure": 91% aren't systematically managing online reputation, letting competitor advantages build over time.

The businesses that address these issues systematically see measurable improvements in 30-60 days. The ones that ignore them watch competitors capture INCREASINGLY market share.

Tools That Make AI Auditing Accessible

You don't need expensive enterprise software to run effective AI audits. Several tools make this process accessible for local businesses:

For Business Listing Management: Tools like BirdEye, Whitespark, and Moz Local use AI to find and monitor your business listings across hundreds of directories.

For Website Technical Analysis: Google's PageSpeed Insights, GTmetrix, and Screaming Frog provide AI-powered technical audits that identify performance issues affecting local search.

For Review Analysis: Reputation management platforms like ReviewTrackers and Grade.us use AI sentiment analysis to identify patterns in customer feedback.

For Local SEO Tracking: BrightLocal, SEMrush, and Ahrefs offer AI-powered local rank tracking that monitors your visibility for thousands of local keyword combinations.

For Competitive Analysis: Tools like SpyFu and SimilarWeb provide AI-driven competitive intelligence showing where competitors get traffic and what strategies work in your market.

Red Flags AI Audits Always Catch

Certain issues appear so frequently in AI audits that they're worth checking manually:

- Phone number variations: Even switching between (555) 123-4567 and 555-123-4567 formats creates confusion
- Address abbreviations: "Street" vs "St" vs "St." inconsistencies across listings
- Category mismatches: Your Google category doesn't match directory categories
- Hours discrepancies: Operating hours listed differently across platforms
- Website/listing disconnects: Your website and business listings tell different stories about services or location

Making AI Audits Work for Your Business

Start with a comprehensive baseline audit, then set up ongoing monitoring to catch issues before they impact your business. The key is systematic attention, not one-time fixes.

Monthly mini-audits using AI tools can catch new problems quickly:

- New negative reviews that need response
- Listing changes that happened without your knowledge
- Technical issues that developed since the last check
- New competitor movements in your market
- Seasonal keyword opportunities you should target

Remember: AI auditing isn't about perfection. It's about continuous improvement and staying ahead of problems that could cost you customers.

The businesses dominating local search aren't necessarily the ones doing everything perfectly. They're the ones who identify and fix issues faster than their competition.

That's the competitive advantage AI auditing provides. The question is: will you use it, or will you let competitors who do pull ahead of you?

Key Insights

"You can't fix what you don't know, AI shows it clearly."
"An audit shouldn't be a chore, it should be a roadmap."
"Local SEO starts with understanding what's invisible."
"AI highlights the cracks, before customers find them."
"Optimization begins in the data."

AI-POWERED KEYWORD STRATEGY FOR LOCAL DOMINATION

Jessica runs a successful lawn care service. For three years, she optimized her website for terms like "lawn care services" and "landscaping company." Her rankings were decent, her website got traffic, but the phone wasn't ringing as much as she expected.

Then we ran an AI analysis of actual search queries in her market.

The results were eye-opening. While Jessica was competing for broad terms with national companies, her potential customers were searching for things like:
- "who can cut my grass tomorrow"
- "lawn service that does edging too"
- "grass cutting near the elementary school"
- "emergency lawn care after storm damage"
- "lawn guy who shows up on time"

These weren't queries Jessica would have thought to target. They sounded too conversational, too specific, too... human.

But here's what the AI revealed: these "conversational" searches were driving 73% more calls than the traditional keywords she'd been targeting. Better yet, almost no local competitors were optimizing for them.

Within two months of creating content around these AI-discovered search terms, Jessica's qualified leads increased 156%. Her phone started ringing with customers who needed exactly what she offered, when she could deliver it.

That's the power of AI keyword research for local businesses. It reveals how people actually search, not how we think they search.

Why Traditional Keyword Research Fails Local Businesses

Most keyword research starts with seed terms and expands from there. You type "plumber" into a tool, get back variations like "emergency plumber" and "residential plumber," then build content around those terms.

This approach misses the reality of modern local search.

Your customers aren't searching like SEO professionals. They're not thinking about keyword difficulty or search volume. They're standing in their flooded basement asking their phone: "who fixes burst pipes right now?"

They're not typing clinical searches like "automotive repair services." They're asking: "why is my car making that grinding noise when I brake?"

Traditional keyword tools show you what people search for across the entire internet. AI-powered local keyword research shows you what your neighbors actually ask when they need what you provide.

The difference is enormous.

The Five Pillars of AI Local Keyword Strategy

1. Local Voice and Long-Tail Searches Are Neighborhood Speak

When people search locally, they use natural language. They include landmarks, neighborhoods, and colloquialisms that make sense in their community but would never show up in national keyword data.

AI tools can analyze local search patterns and reveal terms like:
- "car repair near the mall" (referring to your local shopping center)
- "dentist by the high school" (the landmark everyone knows)
- "pizza delivery to riverside apartments" (the complex everyone calls by that name)
- "handyman who works weekends" (because that's when homeowners need help)

These searches have low national volume but high local intent. More importantly, they have almost no competition because most businesses don't think to target them.

A handyman I worked with discovered that "fix my deck before my party" was searched 40+ times monthly in his area during spring and summer. He created a "last-minute deck repair" service page and captured customers willing to pay premium rates for quick turnaround.

2. AI Tools Analyze Local Search Trends and FAQ Gaps

AI doesn't just find keywords, it identifies patterns in how local customers search and what questions they're not finding good answers to online.

By analyzing search query variations, AI can reveal:
- Seasonal patterns: "AC repair" spikes differently in different climates and communities
- Emergency indicators: Words that signal urgency and willingness to pay premium rates
- Service combinations: How customers bundle services in their searches
- Pain point language: The exact words people use to describe problems
- Time-sensitive searches: When people search for immediate vs. planned services

An HVAC contractor discovered through AI analysis that customers in his area consistently searched for "AC repair same day" but also "AC repair payment plan." This revealed two distinct customer segments: emergency customers who'd pay anything, and budget-conscious customers who needed financing options. He created targeted content for both and increased his qualified leads by 89%.

3. Dynamic Query Discovery Informs Content Strategy

AI keyword research isn't a one-time activity. It's an ongoing discovery process that reveals new opportunities as search behavior evolves.

AI tools can monitor:
- Emerging local search trends before competitors notice them
- New ways customers describe existing problems
- Seasonal shifts in search language and intent
- Questions customers ask but don't find good local answers for
- Voice search evolution as smart speakers become more popular

This dynamic approach means your content strategy evolves with customer behavior instead of relying on outdated assumptions about what people search for.

A restaurant owner used AI monitoring to discover that "takeout family meals under $30" started trending in her area during economic uncertainty. She created a value menu section and captured price-conscious family customers her competitors missed.

4. Low Competition, High Intent Local Query Identification

The best local keywords aren't the ones with highest search volume, they're the ones with highest intent and lowest competition.

AI analysis can identify search terms that are:
- Hyper-specific to your service area: Competitors outside your market can't compete
- High-intent but overlooked: People ready to buy but facing little local competition
- Voice-search optimized: Natural language queries growing as mobile usage increases
- Problem-focused rather than service-focused: How customers describe needs vs. solutions

A locksmith discovered that "locked out of car downtown" got 10x more searches than "automotive locksmith" in his market. He optimized for the natural language version and started getting calls from frustrated customers who needed immediate help rather than people just browsing for future reference.

5. Keyword Intent Layering for Complete Content Planning

AI can categorize local search queries by intent, helping you create content that matches exactly what customers need at each stage:

Immediate Need (Transactional):
- "emergency plumber open now"
- "tow truck available Sunday"
- "dentist appointment today"

Research Phase (Informational):
- "how much does roof repair cost"
- "what causes AC to stop cooling"
- "signs you need brake service"

Comparison Shopping (Commercial):
- "best family restaurant downtown"
- "highest rated auto shop near me"
- "lawn service prices in [area]"

Navigation (Local):
- "[business name] hours"
- "[business name] phone number"
- "directions to [business name]"

Understanding intent helps you create content that matches where customers are in their decision process, INCREASINGLY both rankings and conversions.

The AI Local Keyword Research Process

Here's how to systematically discover and prioritize local keywords using AI:

Phase 1: Seed Term Analysis (30 minutes)

Start with your obvious service terms, but let AI expand them based on actual local search data:
- Input your main services into AI keyword tools
- Include location modifiers relevant to your service area
- Add problem-based variations (what customers experience vs. what you call it)
- Include urgency modifiers (emergency, same day, immediate, etc.)

Phase 2: Competitor Gap Analysis (45 minutes)

Use AI tools to discover what keywords local competitors rank for that you don't:
- Analyze top 5 local competitors' keyword profiles
- Identify high-traffic terms where they're weak or missing
- Find content gaps where customer questions aren't well answered
- Discover local directories or websites driving traffic to competitors

Phase 3: Voice Search Query Discovery (60 minutes)

AI tools can simulate voice searches and reveal conversational query patterns:
- Analyze question-based searches starting with who, what, when, where, why, how
- Identify complete sentence searches people speak to devices
- Find location-specific natural language patterns
- Discover mobile search behavior differences from desktop

Phase 4: Seasonal and Trending Analysis (30 minutes)

AI monitoring reveals when and how search behavior changes:
- Identify seasonal peaks and valleys for different services
- Discover trending topics before they become competitive
- Find weather-related or event-driven search spikes
- Monitor changes in customer language and pain points

Phase 5: Intent Classification and Prioritization (45 minutes)

Organize discovered keywords by business value and optimization opportunity:
- Group by search intent (immediate need vs. research vs. comparison)
- Score by competition level and ranking difficulty
- Prioritize by potential traffic and conversion value
- Create content calendar based on seasonal relevance and business priorities

Turning Keywords Into Content That Converts

Finding the right keywords is only half the battle. The magic happens when you create content that matches both the search query and the customer intent behind it.

For Immediate Need Searches

When someone searches "emergency dentist open Saturday," they don't want a lengthy article about dental health. They want:
- Clear confirmation you're open and available
- Easy contact information prominently displayed
- Simple booking or call-to-action
- Reassurance about emergency services and pain relief

Your content should be scannable, action-oriented, and focused on solving their immediate problem.

For Research Phase Searches

When people search "how much does kitchen remodeling cost," they're in learning mode. They want:
- Detailed information about factors affecting price
- Range examples for different project types
- Process explanation so they understand what's involved
- Trust signals showing your expertise and reliability

This content can be longer and more educational, positioning you as the expert they'll call when they're ready to move forward.

For Comparison Searches

When customers search "best Italian restaurant downtown," they're evaluating options. They want:
- Clear differentiation from competitors
- Social proof through reviews and testimonials
- Specific details about what makes you special
- Easy way to take the next step (reservation, directions, menu)

Local Keyword Research Tools That Work

Several AI-powered tools make local keyword research accessible and actionable:

AnswerThePublic: Uses AI to find question-based searches people ask about your services in your area.

Also Asked: Discovers "People Also Ask" questions from Google search results, revealing customer curiosity gaps.

SEMrush Local: Provides AI-powered local keyword analysis showing what works in your specific market.

BrightLocal: Offers local search insights including voice search query analysis and competitor keyword gaps.

Google's Keyword Planner: When filtered for local areas, reveals actual search volume and competition for location-specific terms.

Ubersuggest: Neil Patel's tool includes local keyword suggestions with difficulty scores and content ideas.

Voice Search: The Future of Local Keywords

Voice search is growing rapidly, especially for local queries. People ask their phones and smart speakers for local business recommendations more than any other type of voice search.

AI analysis of voice searches reveals different patterns than text searches:

Text Search: "Italian restaurants downtown" Voice Search: "Where can I get good Italian food for dinner tonight?"

Text Search: "emergency plumber" Voice Search: "Who can fix a burst pipe right now?"

Text Search: "auto repair shop" Voice Search: "My car won't start, who can help me?"

Optimizing for voice search means creating content that answers complete questions in natural, conversational language.

Common Local Keyword Mistakes AI Helps You Avoid

The Generic Trap: Competing for broad terms where national companies dominate instead of specific local queries where you can win.

The Volume Obsession: Chasing high-volume keywords instead of high-intent searches that actually drive business.

The SEO Speak Problem: Optimizing for how marketers talk instead of how customers actually search.

The Set-It-and-Forget-It Error: Using outdated keyword research instead of adapting to changing search behavior.

The Voice Search Blindness: Ignoring conversational queries that drive INCREASINGLY mobile traffic.

Measuring Local Keyword Success

Track metrics that matter for local business:

Rankings: Position for target keywords, especially in Maps results Traffic: Visitors from organic local search, segmented by device and intent Calls: Phone calls attributed to specific keyword rankings Conversions: Form submissions, appointments, or other goal completions Revenue: Actual business generated from organic search traffic

The goal isn't just rankings, it's profitable customers who found you through search.

Building Your Local Keyword Strategy

Start with a comprehensive AI-powered keyword audit, then build content systematically:

1. Month 1: Target immediate-need, high-intent keywords where you can rank quickly
2. Month 2: Create educational content for research-phase searches
3. Month 3: Develop comparison content that differentiates you from competitors
4. Month 4+: Expand into seasonal, trending, and voice search opportunities

Remember: the best local keyword strategy isn't about ranking for everything. It's about ranking for searches that bring you the right customers at the right time.

Your competitors are still optimizing for generic terms that worked five years ago. While they fight over broad keywords with national companies, you can dominate the specific, conversational searches that drive local business.

AI gives you the insights to find those opportunities. The question is: will you use them to pull ahead, or will you keep competing where everyone else is already fighting?

Key Insights

"Your keywords should speak like a neighbor, not a marketer."
"AI knows what locals ask, listen."
"No more guessing, AI surfaces what people really type."
"Long-tail isn't long, it's precise."
"Your content strategy starts with listening, not writing."

GENERATING GEO-TARGETED CONTENT AT SCALE

David owns a therapy practice that serves five different neighborhoods in his metro area. Each area has its own character, different demographics, income levels, and community concerns. For years, he'd been creating generic content about therapy services, hoping it would appeal to everyone.

The results were predictably mediocre. His website got some traffic, but conversion rates were low and most inquiries came from people who weren't a good fit for his practice.

Then we implemented an AI-powered geo-targeted content strategy.

Instead of generic articles about "managing anxiety," David started publishing content like:
- "Supporting Working Parents in Riverside: Managing Stress When School Schedules Change"
- "Mental Health Resources Near Downtown Metro Station: Evening Appointments Available"
- "Coping with Job Market Changes: Career Counseling for Tech Workers in Innovation District"

Each piece of content spoke directly to the specific concerns and situations of people in different parts of his service area. The content felt personal and relevant because it was written for specific communities, not generic audiences.

The results were immediate. Within three months, David's website traffic increased 89%. More importantly, his consultation requests jumped 214%, and the quality of inquiries improved dramatically. People were calling specifically because they'd found content that addressed their exact situation in their exact neighborhood.

That's what happens when you stop creating content for "everyone" and start creating content for someone specific. AI makes it possible to do this at scale without burning out your content team.

Why Generic Content Fails Local Businesses

Most local businesses approach content creation backwards. They start with their services and try to write about them in ways that appeal to the broadest possible audience.

This creates content that sounds like it was written by a committee:
- "Our dental practice provides comprehensive oral health services for families"
- "We offer reliable plumbing solutions for residential and commercial clients"
- "Experience professional landscaping services tailored to your needs"

This language doesn't connect with anyone because it's trying to connect with everyone.

Your potential customers aren't looking for "comprehensive solutions" or "professional services." They're dealing with specific problems in specific places:

- "My kid is terrified of the dentist and we live near the elementary school"
- "The toilet in our downtown apartment won't stop running"
- "Our front yard looks terrible compared to the rest of the subdivision"

Geo-targeted content addresses real people with real problems in real places. It converts better because it feels more relevant and trustworthy.

The Five Pillars of AI Geo-Targeted Content

1. AI Helps Draft Content; Human Edits Keep Tone Local and Authentic

The biggest misconception about AI content creation is that it replaces human creativity. In reality, AI handles the heavy lifting so humans can focus on what they do best, adding personality, local knowledge, and authentic voice.

Here's how the process works:

AI handles: Research, structure, first drafts, keyword optimization, and content variations Humans handle: Local references, community knowledge, brand voice, personal stories, and final polish

An accountant I worked with used AI to create tax preparation content for different neighborhoods in her city. The AI generated solid frameworks about tax deadlines and deduction strategies. She added specific details about local businesses that qualified for certain deductions, references to community events that created tax implications, and stories from actual clients in each area.

The result was content that felt both professionally comprehensive and locally personal.

2. Geo-Specific References Increase Relevance

When you mention local landmarks, neighborhoods, schools, or businesses in your content, search engines recognize it as locally relevant. More importantly, readers immediately know you understand their community.

Instead of: "Many families struggle with work-life balance" Try: "With the new corporate campus bringing 3,000+ jobs to Riverside, many families are adjusting to longer commutes and different schedules"

Instead of: "Our restaurant serves fresh, local ingredients" Try: "We source produce from Miller's Farm Market every Tuesday and get fresh bread daily from the bakery on Main Street"

AI can help identify these local reference opportunities by analyzing:

- Local news websites and community blogs
- Social media conversations in your area
- Review mentions of local landmarks and businesses
- Community calendar events and recurring activities
- Local government announcements and city planning news

3. Repurposable Templates Scale Content Creation

The key to geo-targeted content at scale is creating templates that AI can adapt for different locations while maintaining local relevance.

For example, a "Best Of" template might include:

- Introduction acknowledging the specific neighborhood
- 5-7 local businesses or attractions
- Personal experience or customer stories from that area
- Call-to-action specific to that location's needs

AI can populate this template with research about different neighborhoods, then you customize it with personal knowledge and local voice.

A real estate agent used this approach to create "Living in [Neighborhood]" guides for 12 different areas. AI handled the demographic research, school ratings, and housing market data. She added insights about community character, local events, and why different types of buyers loved each area.

Instead of spending weeks researching and writing, she produced comprehensive neighborhood guides in days.

4. AI-Driven Variation Prevents Duplicate Content

One challenge with geo-targeted content is avoiding duplicate content penalties while covering similar topics for different areas.

AI excels at creating meaningful variations that satisfy both search engines and readers:

- Different angles on similar topics
- Varied content structures and formats
- Unique examples and case studies for each location
- Different seasonal or timing considerations
- Varied calls-to-action based on local needs

A home services contractor created seasonal maintenance content for different neighborhoods using AI variation. Each area got genuinely different content based on local factors:

- Coastal areas: saltwater corrosion and humidity considerations
- Hill country: drainage and foundation issues
- New developments: builder warranty and landscaping tips
- Historic districts: maintaining older systems and architectural integrity

5. Micro-Local Pages Serve Distinct Searcher Intent

The most effective geo-targeted content creates specific pages for specific search intents in specific locations.

Instead of one page about "emergency dental services," create:

- "Emergency Dentist Downtown: Open Evenings and Weekends"
- "Children's Emergency Dental Care Near Elementary Schools"
- "After-Hours Dental Emergencies: Westside Location"

Each page serves different searcher intent while targeting location-specific queries that competitors miss.

The AI Geo-Content Creation Process

Phase 1: Market Research and Template Development (Week 1)

Use AI to analyze your service area and identify distinct neighborhoods or customer segments:

- Demographic analysis of different areas you serve
- Local search volume for services in each area
- Community-specific concerns and interests
- Seasonal patterns that vary by location
- Competitor content gaps in specific areas

Create content templates that can be adapted for different locations while maintaining uniqueness.

Phase 2: Content Calendar Planning (Week 2)

Develop a systematic approach to covering all your service areas:

- Assign content themes to specific neighborhoods
- Plan seasonal content that varies by area
- Schedule community event tie-ins
- Balance educational and promotional content
- Coordinate with local marketing activities

Phase 3: AI-Powered Content Generation (Ongoing)

Use AI to create first drafts while maintaining quality standards:
- Generate content outlines based on local keyword research
- Create multiple variations of similar topics for different areas
- Develop FAQ content addressing location-specific concerns
- Build resource lists and guides for each neighborhood
- Automate basic research while preserving editorial control

Phase 4: Local Customization and Publishing (Ongoing)

Add the local knowledge and authentic voice that AI can't provide:
- Insert specific local references and landmarks
- Add personal stories and client examples from each area
- Include location-specific calls-to-action
- Optimize for locally relevant keywords and phrases
- Schedule publication to align with local events or seasons

Content Types That Work Best for Geo-Targeting

Neighborhood Guides and Area Spotlights

Create comprehensive resources about specific areas you serve:
- "Living in [Neighborhood]: A Complete Guide"
- "Best Family Activities in [Area]"
- "[Neighborhood] Business Directory"
- "What to Expect When Moving to [Area]"

Service Area-Specific Landing Pages

Optimize individual pages for location-based searches:
- "[Service] in [Neighborhood]"
- "Emergency [Service] Near [Landmark]"
- "[Neighborhood] [Business Type]"
- "Best [Service] in [Area]"

Local Event and News Tie-Ins

Connect your expertise to local happenings:
- "Preparing Your Home for [Local Weather Pattern]"
- "How [Local Development] Affects Property Values"
- "Supporting Local Health During [Seasonal Challenge]"
- "[Local Event] Planning Tips from a Local Expert"

Community Problem-Solving Content

Address issues specific to different areas:
- "Dealing with [Area-Specific Problem]"
- "Why [Neighborhood] Residents Choose [Your Solution]"
- "Local Solutions for [Community Challenge]"
- "Understanding [Area] Regulations and Requirements"

Avoiding Common Geo-Content Pitfalls

The Keyword Stuffing Trap

Don't force location names into every sentence. Use them naturally when they add value:

Bad: "Our downtown plumbers provide downtown plumbing services for downtown businesses and downtown residents in the downtown area."

Good: "When pipes burst in older downtown buildings, quick response time matters. We're located three blocks from the business district and can typically arrive within 15 minutes."

The Generic Template Problem

Avoid content that's obviously templated by varying:
- Writing style and structure
- Examples and case studies
- Calls-to-action and next steps
- Seasonal references and timing
- Local knowledge and insights

The Authenticity Gap

Don't write about areas you don't know. If you're creating content for locations you haven't personally experienced:
- Visit the area and take notes
- Interview customers from that neighborhood
- Research local news and community discussions
- Partner with local businesses or organizations
- Be honest about your connection to the area

Measuring Geo-Content Success

Track performance metrics that matter for local content:

Search Rankings: Position for location-specific keywords Local Traffic: Visitors from specific geographic areas Engagement: Time on page and bounce rate by location Conversions: Leads and customers from different areas Social Shares: Community engagement with location-specific content

Use this data to refine your geo-targeting strategy and focus on what works best in each area.

Tools for Scaling Geo-Targeted Content

Content Research: BuzzSumo, AnswerThePublic, and Google Trends for local content ideas AI Writing: Jasper, Copy.ai, and Writesonic for content generation and variation Local Data: Census data, local government websites, and community forums for area-specific information SEO Optimization: Clearscope and MarketMuse for local keyword integration Performance Tracking: Google Analytics and local rank tracking tools for measuring results

Building Your Geo-Content Strategy

Start small and scale systematically:

Month 1: Create content for your highest-value service area Month 2: Expand to 2-3 additional neighborhoods Month 3: Add seasonal and event-based content Month 4: Develop ongoing content calendar covering all service areas

Focus on quality over quantity. Better to create excellent content for a few areas than mediocre content for many.

The Competitive Advantage of Local Relevance

While your competitors create generic content hoping to appeal to everyone, you can dominate specific local searches with content that speaks directly to community needs.

This isn't just about SEO, it's about building genuine connections with your community. When people find content that addresses their specific situation in their specific area, they don't just visit your website. They remember you as the business that "gets it."

AI makes this level of personalization scalable. You can create content that feels personally relevant to different neighborhoods without spending weeks researching each area.

The businesses that master geo-targeted content don't just get more traffic, they get better traffic. Customers who are more likely to convert because the content spoke directly to their situation.

Your competitors are still creating one-size-fits-all content. While they fight for attention in the broad marketplace, you can own the specific local conversations that matter most to your ideal customers.

Key Insights

"Local content isn't everywhere, it's right here."
"AI drafts, you localize."
"Scale doesn't mean generic, it means varied and relevant."
"Location-based content bridges digital to doorstep."
"Write once, adapt everywhere, smartly."

AI-POWERED GOOGLE BUSINESS PROFILE OPTIMIZATION

Maria thought her restaurant's Google Business Profile was "good enough." She had photos, operating hours, and her menu posted. Customer reviews were decent. When people searched for restaurants in her area, she occasionally appeared in the Map Pack.

But "occasionally" wasn't building the business she wanted.

Then we ran an AI analysis of her Google Business Profile performance compared to local competitors. The results revealed opportunities Maria never knew existed.

AI discovered that posts with specific food photos got 340% more clicks than generic restaurant shots. It identified that customers were asking the same five questions repeatedly in reviews, but Maria's profile didn't address any of them. The analysis showed that her main competitor was posting updates 3x more frequently, keeping their profile fresh and engaged.

Most surprisingly, AI found that 67% of searches for restaurants in her area included time-sensitive terms like "open now" or "dinner tonight," but Maria's profile wasn't optimized for these real-time queries.

We implemented an AI-powered Google Business Profile strategy that addressed every gap:
- Automated posting schedule with food photos and daily specials
- Q&A section that proactively answered the most common customer questions
- Real-time updates about availability, wait times, and special offers
- Photo optimization with local keywords and menu item descriptions
- Review response templates that maintained personal voice while ensuring consistency

Within 60 days, Maria's restaurant went from occasionally appearing in local search to dominating the Map Pack for dinner searches. Her Google profile clicks increased 156%, phone calls jumped 89%, and most importantly, foot traffic grew enough that she had to hire additional staff.

That's what happens when you treat your Google Business Profile like the dynamic marketing tool it is, instead of a static online listing.

Why Most Google Business Profiles Underperform

The majority of local businesses set up their Google Business Profile once and forget about it. They add basic information, upload a few photos, and hope customers find them.

This "set it and forget it" approach misses the reality of how Google's local search algorithm works. Google favors profiles that are:

- Active: Regular posts and updates show you're engaged with customers
- Complete: Every section filled out with relevant, keyword-rich information
- Responsive: Quick replies to reviews and questions build trust signals
- Fresh: New photos and content indicate an active, current business
- Engaging: High click-through rates and customer interactions boost visibility

Your Google Business Profile isn't just a listing, it's a dynamic marketing platform that can drive significant business when optimized correctly.

The Five Pillars of AI-Powered Google Business Profile Optimization

1. Dynamic Content Recommendations Keep Your Profile Active

AI analysis of successful local businesses reveals posting patterns that drive engagement:

- Daily specials and offers: Posts about current promotions get 3x more clicks
- Behind-the-scenes content: Photos of staff, kitchen, or work processes build trust
- Customer spotlights: Featuring happy customers encourages others to visit
- Educational content: Quick tips related to your industry position you as an expert
- Event announcements: Local events and special hours capture timely searches

AI can analyze your industry and location to suggest content that performs well for similar businesses in your area. It can even generate post ideas based on seasonal trends, local events, and competitor analysis.

A home services contractor used AI recommendations to post regularly about:

- Seasonal maintenance tips before weather changes
- Before/after project photos with local neighborhood references
- Customer testimonials from different service areas
- Emergency service availability during storms
- Educational content about common home problems

His profile engagement increased 127% and emergency service calls doubled during peak seasons.

2. Photo and Video Optimization Increases Local Search Relevance

Most businesses upload random photos without considering how AI analyzes visual content for local relevance. Google's image recognition can identify:

- Specific products and services in your photos
- Local landmarks and neighborhood characteristics
- Professional quality and authenticity indicators
- Seasonal relevance and timing appropriateness
- Customer engagement and satisfaction cues

AI-powered photo optimization means:

Strategic naming: Instead of "IMG_1234.jpg," use "downtown-italian-restaurant-pasta-special.jpg" Geo-tagged locations: Photos tagged with your business location signal local relevance Keyword-rich descriptions: Photo captions that include local search terms and service descriptions Optimal timing: Posting photos when your target customers are most active online Consistent branding: Visual consistency across all profile images builds recognition

A dentist optimized her profile photos using AI insights:
- Treatment room photos tagged with "comfortable dental office downtown"
- Before/after photos described as "cosmetic dentistry results local patients"
- Staff photos captioned with "friendly dental team serving families since 2015"
- Technology photos highlighting "advanced dental equipment for pain-free procedures"

Her profile views increased 91% and new patient inquiries grew 34%.

3. AI Sentiment Analysis Improves Review Management

Managing reviews manually means you're always reactive. AI sentiment analysis helps you become proactive by identifying:
- Review themes that appear across multiple customers
- Service issues mentioned repeatedly that need operational fixes
- Strengths customers highlight that should be emphasized in marketing
- Response opportunities where thoughtful replies can demonstrate excellent service
- Trending concerns before they become bigger reputation problems

AI can also suggest response templates that maintain your brand voice while addressing common review situations:

Positive reviews: Thank customers while highlighting specific services they mentioned Negative reviews: Acknowledge concerns, offer solutions, and invite offline resolution Neutral reviews: Add value by providing additional helpful information

A veterinary clinic used AI review analysis to discover that 73% of negative reviews mentioned "long wait times." Instead of just responding to reviews, they implemented an appointment reminder system and waiting room improvements. New reviews started highlighting their "efficient service" and "minimal wait times."

4. Smart Posting Based on Customer Demand Signals

AI can analyze when your customers are most likely to search for your services and schedule posts accordingly:
- Seasonal patterns: HVAC companies post about heating before cold snaps
- Weekly cycles: Restaurants promote weekend specials on Thursday-Friday
- Daily timing: Coffee shops post morning specials at 7 AM when commuters check their phones
- Event-driven: Landscapers post storm cleanup services when weather alerts are issued

This timing optimization can dramatically improve post visibility and engagement.

A tax preparation service used AI to identify that most people search for tax help on Sunday evenings and Monday mornings, when they're thinking about the upcoming week. By scheduling posts for Sunday at 7 PM, their engagement rates increased 89%.

5. Automated Optimization Maintains Consistent Performance

The most successful Google Business Profiles aren't managed sporadically, they're optimized consistently. AI can automate many optimization tasks:

Content scheduling: Regular posts keep your profile active without manual effort Photo rotation: Fresh images uploaded automatically based on performance data Q&A updates: Common questions answered proactively based on customer inquiries Hours adjustments: Automatic updates for holidays and special events Competitor monitoring: Alerts when competitors make profile changes you should consider

This consistent activity signals to Google that your business is active and engaged, improving your local search visibility.

The AI Google Business Profile Optimization Process

Phase 1: Profile Audit and Baseline Assessment (Week 1)

Use AI tools to analyze your current profile performance:
- Completeness scoring: Identify missing information and optimization opportunities
- Photo analysis: Evaluate current images for local relevance and engagement potential
- Competitor benchmarking: Compare your profile to successful local competitors
- Keyword analysis: Review how well your profile targets relevant local searches
- Engagement metrics: Assess current click-through rates, calls, and direction requests

Phase 2: Content Strategy Development (Week 2)

Create an AI-informed content plan:
- Posting calendar: Schedule regular updates based on customer search patterns
- Photo strategy: Plan visual content that showcases services and builds local connections
- Q&A preparation: Develop answers for common customer questions
- Review response templates: Create consistent but personalized response frameworks
- Seasonal adjustments: Plan content that aligns with business cycles and local events

Phase 3: Implementation and Automation Setup (Week 3-4)

Deploy AI-powered optimization systems:
- Automated posting: Schedule regular content updates
- Photo optimization: Implement proper naming and tagging strategies
- Review monitoring: Set up alerts for new reviews and response opportunities
- Performance tracking: Monitor profile analytics and engagement metrics
- Competitor alerts: Track changes in local competition

Phase 4: Ongoing Optimization and Refinement (Monthly)

Use AI insights to continuously improve profile performance:
- Performance analysis: Review what content drives the most engagement
- Strategy adjustments: Adapt posting frequency and content types based on results
- New opportunity identification: Discover emerging local search trends
- Competitive responses: Adjust strategy based on competitor activities
- Seasonal preparations: Update content and information for upcoming seasons

Google Business Profile Features That Drive Results

Posts That Convert

AI analysis shows certain post types consistently outperform others:

Offer posts: Specific discounts or promotions with clear calls-to-action Event posts: Announcements about sales, open houses, or special services Product posts: Featured services or seasonal offerings Update posts: Business news, new services, or operational changes

Each post type serves different customer intents and search behaviors.

Q&A Optimization

Proactively answer questions customers ask:
- Service availability: Hours, emergency services, appointment scheduling
- Pricing information: General cost ranges, consultation fees, payment options
- Location details: Parking, accessibility, nearby landmarks
- Process questions: How services work, what to expect, preparation needed
- Qualification criteria: Who you serve, service area limitations, specialization focus

Strategic Category Selection
Choose primary and secondary categories that match customer search behavior:

Primary category: Your main business type as customers would search for it Secondary categories: Additional services that capture related searches Avoid over-categorization: Too many categories can dilute your primary focus Update seasonally: Add temporary categories for seasonal services

Common Google Business Profile Mistakes AI Helps You Avoid

The Information Inconsistency Problem

AI auditing catches discrepancies between your profile and other online listings:
- Phone number variations across platforms
- Address formatting differences
- Business name inconsistencies
- Hours that don't match your website
- Service descriptions that contradict other marketing

The Generic Content Trap

Avoid posts that could apply to any business:
- "We provide quality service" (everyone says this)
- "Customer satisfaction is our priority" (meaningless without specifics)
- "Call us for all your needs" (doesn't indicate what you do)

The Photo Quality Problem

AI can identify photos that hurt rather than help your profile:
- Blurry or poorly lit images
- Photos that don't show your actual business
- Outdated images that don't reflect current services
- Generic stock photos instead of authentic business shots

Tools for AI-Powered Google Business Profile Management

BirdEye: AI-powered reputation management with automated review responses and profile optimization Hootsuite: Social media scheduling that includes Google Business Profile posting ReviewTrackers: AI sentiment analysis and review management automation LocalClarity: Google Business Profile analytics and optimization recommendations Chatmeter: Multi-location profile management with AI-driven insights

Measuring Google Business Profile Success

Track metrics that indicate real business impact:

Visibility Metrics:
- Search appearances for target keywords
- Map Pack inclusion frequency
- Profile views and photo views

Engagement Metrics:
- Click-through rates to website
- Phone calls from profile
- Direction requests
- Message inquiries

Conversion Metrics:
- Leads generated from profile traffic
- Appointments booked through profile
- Revenue attributed to local search

Competitive Metrics:
- Ranking position vs. competitors
- Review quantity and quality comparison
- Profile completeness vs. competition

Building Your AI-Powered Profile Strategy

Week 1: Complete profile audit and competitive analysis Week 2: Implement missing information and optimize existing content Week 3: Launch automated posting and monitoring systems Week 4: Begin review management and Q&A optimization Month 2+: Refine strategy based on performance data and customer feedback

The Competitive Edge of AI Optimization

While most local businesses treat their Google Business Profile as a static listing, AI-powered optimization turns it into a dynamic lead-generation engine.

You're not just listing your business information, you're creating an engaging, always-current showcase that captures customers when they're ready to buy.

Your competitors are posting randomly when they remember to. You're posting strategically when customers are most likely to search.

They're responding to reviews reactively. You're managing reputation proactively.

They're guessing what customers want to know. You're answering the questions data shows customers actually ask.

This isn't just about better rankings, it's about creating a profile that converts browsers into customers at a higher rate than your competition.

The local businesses dominating Google search aren't necessarily the biggest or oldest. They're the ones that understand how AI can optimize every aspect of their online presence for maximum customer attraction and conversion.

Key Insights

"Your Google Business Profile is your local storefront, keep it tidy with AI."
"Reviews tell stories, AI helps you choose which ones you amplify."
"An optimized profile is a signal to search engines, not just a listing."
"AI keeps your profile alive, not just accurate."
"Local SEO is local trust, AI helps you demonstrate it."

SMART REVIEW FUNNELS AND REPUTATION MANAGEMENT

Tom runs a successful auto repair shop that consistently delivers excellent service. His customers love the work, trust his recommendations, and come back year after year. But when potential customers searched for auto repair online, Tom's business was invisible.

The problem wasn't his service quality, it was his review strategy. Or rather, his complete lack of one.

Tom had 23 five-star reviews scattered across Google, Yelp, and Facebook over three years. His main competitor, who frankly didn't do work as good as Tom's, had 847 reviews and dominated local search results.

"I don't want to bother customers for reviews," Tom told me. "Good work should speak for itself."

I explained that in the digital age, good work only speaks for itself if customers can hear it. And they can't hear it if it's not online where they're looking.

We implemented an AI-powered review management system that transformed Tom's approach:

- Automated timing that requested reviews when customers were happiest
- Sentiment analysis that identified which customers were most likely to leave positive reviews
- Smart filtering that directed happy customers to public review sites and concerned customers to private feedback channels
- Response templates that maintained Tom's authentic voice while ensuring consistent, professional replies
- Review monitoring that caught new feedback within hours instead of days

The results were dramatic. Within four months, Tom's review count increased from 23 to 312. More importantly, review quality improved, customers started writing detailed testimonials about specific services and experiences.

His local search rankings jumped from page 2 to the top 3 for major keywords. Phone calls increased 156%. Revenue grew 34% as higher online visibility brought in customers who previously would have gone to competitors.

Tom learned that asking for reviews isn't bothering customers, it's giving satisfied customers a way to help other people find great service.

Why Most Local Businesses Fail at Review Management

The majority of local businesses approach online reviews passively. They hope customers will leave reviews, respond when they remember to, and cross their fingers that good reviews outweigh bad ones.

This passive approach fails because:

Timing matters: Most customers forget to leave reviews unless prompted at the right moment Happy customers are quiet: Satisfied customers rarely think to share their experience online Unhappy customers are loud: Frustrated customers are more motivated to write reviews than happy ones Review platforms vary: Different customers prefer different review sites Response speed impacts perception: Slow responses to negative reviews make problems look ignored

AI-powered review management flips this dynamic. Instead of hoping for good reviews and reacting to bad ones, you proactively build review acquisition systems and manage reputation strategically.

The Five Pillars of AI-Powered Review Management

1. AI Clustering Identifies Recurring Themes and Patterns

When you have dozens or hundreds of reviews, patterns become impossible to spot manually. AI can analyze all your reviews and identify:

Positive themes: What customers consistently praise about your business
- "Fast service" mentioned in 67% of reviews
- "Fair pricing" highlighted by 43% of customers
- "Knowledgeable staff" appears in 58% of testimonials

Negative patterns: Issues that come up repeatedly
- "Long wait times" mentioned in 23% of negative reviews
- "Parking difficulties" noted by 15% of customers
- "Communication delays" cited in multiple reviews

Service-specific feedback: How customers rate different aspects of your business
- Installation services: 4.8/5 average with "professional" mentioned frequently
- Customer service: 4.2/5 with "helpful" and "patient" as common themes
- Pricing: 4.1/5 with mixed feedback on "value" vs. "expensive"

A medical practice used AI review analysis to discover that 78% of positive reviews mentioned their appointment scheduling system, while 65% of negative reviews complained about wait times. They restructured their scheduling process and updated their online booking system. New reviews started highlighting "efficient appointments" instead of criticizing delays.

2. Dynamic Response Suggestions Maintain Voice While Ensuring Consistency

Responding to reviews manually often results in:
- Delayed responses that make you look inattentive
- Inconsistent tone across different team members
- Generic responses that don't address specific feedback
- Missed opportunities to highlight your strengths

AI can generate response suggestions that:
- Match your established brand voice and tone
- Address specific points mentioned in each review
- Include relevant business information (services, policies, contact details)
- Vary language to avoid looking robotic or templated
- Escalate complex issues for human review

A restaurant used AI-suggested responses to maintain consistency while personalizing each reply:

For positive reviews: Thank customers by name, mention specific dishes they enjoyed, invite them back for seasonal specials

For negative reviews: Acknowledge specific concerns, explain any misunderstandings, offer to discuss solutions offline

For neutral reviews: Add value by providing additional information about services or improvements since their visit

Response time improved from 3-5 days to under 4 hours, and customers began commenting on the "attentive management" in subsequent reviews.

3. Automated Review Solicitation Based on Customer Satisfaction Signals

The key to getting more positive reviews is asking the right customers at the right time. AI can identify optimal review request timing by analyzing:

Service completion signals: Automated requests sent after successful project completion Customer satisfaction indicators: Follow-up surveys that gauge satisfaction before requesting public reviews Communication patterns: Positive email exchanges or phone conversations that indicate happy customers Purchase behavior: Repeat customers or referrals who demonstrate satisfaction Timing optimization: Days and times when customers are most likely to respond to review requests

A home services company implemented smart review timing:
- Immediate requests after emergency services (customers grateful for quick response)
- 48-hour delay after major installations (allows time to appreciate the work)
- One-week follow-up for routine maintenance (ensures everything is working properly)
- Seasonal requests for past customers when services are top-of-mind

Their review response rate increased from 12% to 47%, and review quality improved as they were capturing customers at peak satisfaction moments.

4. Alert Systems for Reputation Issues Before They Escalate

AI monitoring can catch potential reputation problems early:

Sentiment shifts: Detecting when review sentiment trends negative before it becomes a pattern Competitor monitoring: Alerts when competitors are gaining review advantages Platform performance: Tracking which review sites are most important for your visibility Review velocity changes: Noticing when review acquisition slows or spikes unexpectedly Crisis detection: Identifying when negative reviews require immediate attention

A dental practice received an AI alert when three negative reviews in one week all mentioned "rushed appointments." They investigated and discovered that an overpacked schedule was causing staff to hurry patients. They adjusted scheduling to allow more time per appointment, preventing additional negative reviews and improving patient satisfaction.

5. Positive Review Amplification for Marketing Content

Your best reviews contain powerful marketing content that AI can help you leverage:

Testimonial extraction: Identifying the most compelling customer quotes for marketing materials Service validation: Reviews that confirm your key selling points and differentiators SEO content: Customer language that matches how prospects search for your services Case study material: Detailed reviews that tell complete customer success stories Social proof: Reviews that address common objections or concerns prospects have

An accounting firm used AI to analyze their reviews and discovered customers frequently mentioned "stress relief" and "peace of mind" when describing their tax preparation experience. They incorporated this language into their marketing, resulting in 23% higher conversion rates on their tax services landing page.

The AI Review Management Process

Phase 1: Current State Analysis (Week 1)
Assess your existing review profile across all platforms:
- Review inventory: Count and analyze reviews across Google, Yelp, Facebook, industry-specific sites
- Sentiment analysis: Identify positive themes, negative patterns, and neutral feedback opportunities
- Competitive benchmarking: Compare your review profile to local competitors
- Platform performance: Determine which review sites drive the most customer traffic
- Response audit: Evaluate current review response strategy and timing

Phase 2: Review Acquisition System Setup (Week 2)
Build automated systems for generating more reviews:

- Customer journey mapping: Identify optimal moments for review requests
- Multi-channel approach: Set up review requests via email, text, and in-person prompts
- Platform selection: Direct different customers to their preferred review platforms
- Request timing: Automate review requests based on service completion and satisfaction signals
- Follow-up sequences: Create gentle reminder systems for customers who don't respond initially

Phase 3: Response Strategy Implementation (Week 3)
Develop consistent, effective review response processes:

- Response templates: Create AI-suggested responses that maintain your authentic voice
- Escalation procedures: Define when reviews require human attention vs. automated responses
- Timing goals: Set response time targets (ideally under 24 hours for all reviews)
- Team training: Ensure all staff understand review response protocols
- Quality control: Regular audits of review responses to maintain brand standards

Phase 4: Ongoing Monitoring and Optimization (Monthly)
Use AI insights to continuously improve review performance:

- Performance tracking: Monitor review acquisition rates, sentiment trends, and platform performance
- Strategy refinement: Adjust timing, messaging, and platforms based on results
- Competitive monitoring: Stay aware of competitor review strategies and performance
- Content harvesting: Identify and leverage positive reviews for marketing materials
- Issue prevention: Address recurring negative themes before they become larger problems

Review Platform Strategy

Different customers prefer different review platforms. AI can help you optimize for each:

Google Business Profile

- Primary focus: Most important for local search visibility
- Customer behavior: People search Google first for local businesses
- Optimization: Encourage reviews from customers who found you through search
- Response priority: Fastest response times needed due to high visibility

Industry-Specific Platforms
- Targeted relevance: HomeAdvisor for contractors, Healthgrades for medical, etc.
- Customer expectations: Users expect to find you on industry platforms
- Higher conversion: Prospects using industry sites are further in the buying process
- Detailed feedback: Industry platforms often allow more comprehensive reviews

Social Media Reviews
- Facebook: Good for local businesses with strong community connections
- LinkedIn: Important for B2B services and professional credibility
- Platform-specific: Instagram, TikTok for businesses with visual appeal

General Review Sites
- Yelp: Still important in many markets, especially for restaurants and consumer services
- Better Business Bureau: Credibility for larger purchases and professional services

Advanced Review Strategies

The Review Funnel Approach

Not every customer should be asked for public reviews immediately:

Stage 1 - Satisfaction Check: Private feedback opportunity to identify issues Stage 2 - Happy Customer Routing: Direct satisfied customers to public review platforms Stage 3 - Issue Resolution: Address concerns privately before they become public reviews Stage 4 - Follow-up: Request public reviews after resolving any issues

Seasonal Review Campaigns

AI can identify when your customers are most likely to need and appreciate your services:
- Tax accountants: Request reviews in April-May when service is fresh in customers' minds
- HVAC services: Ask for reviews after successful emergency repairs during extreme weather
- Landscapers: Time review requests with completed seasonal projects
- Retailers: Coordinate review requests with peak shopping seasons

Review Response SEO
Your review responses are public content that search engines index:
- Keyword integration: Naturally include relevant keywords in responses
- Service mentions: Reference specific services when thanking customers
- Location references: Mention neighborhoods or areas when relevant
- Call-to-action: Include contact information for prospects reading responses

Common Review Management Mistakes

The "Set It and Forget It" Error

Automated systems need regular monitoring and adjustment based on performance data.

The Generic Response Problem

Template responses that don't address specific customer comments look robotic and uncaring.

The Platform Neglect Issue

Focusing only on Google while ignoring industry-specific or niche review platforms where your ideal customers research.

The Defensive Response Trap

Arguing with negative reviewers publicly instead of taking conversations offline for resolution.

The Review Request Timing Mistake

Asking for reviews immediately after service instead of waiting for optimal satisfaction moments.

Measuring Review Management Success
Track metrics that indicate real business impact:

Volume Metrics:
- Total reviews acquired monthly
- Review velocity compared to competitors
- Platform distribution of new reviews

Quality Metrics:
- Average star rating trends
- Review length and detail quality
- Percentage of reviews mentioning specific services

Business Impact Metrics:
- Local search ranking improvements
- Website traffic from review sites
- Phone calls and leads attributed to reviews
- Conversion rate of prospects who mention finding you through reviews

Response Metrics:

- Average response time to reviews
- Percentage of reviews receiving responses
- Customer satisfaction with review responses

Building Your Review Management System

Month 1: Analyze current reviews and set up automated acquisition systems

Month 2: Implement response strategies and begin consistent review monitoring

Month 3: Optimize timing and messaging based on initial results

Month 4+: Scale successful tactics and explore advanced reputation management strategies

Remember: review management isn't about manipulation, it's about systematically giving happy customers easy ways to share their experiences and ensuring all customers feel heard and valued.

Your competitors are still hoping customers will remember to leave reviews. While they wait passively, you can build systems that consistently generate positive reviews from satisfied customers.

The businesses that dominate local search aren't necessarily the ones with perfect service, they're the ones that make it easy for satisfied customers to share their experiences and handle negative feedback professionally.

AI makes this systematic approach accessible to any local business willing to invest in their online reputation.

Key Insights

"Your reviews are your reputation's pulse, AI reads it in real time."
"You can't ask manually, AI asks with context and timing."
"Negative trends are opportunities to improve, if spotted early."
"Happy customers make the best advocates, AI identifies who they are."
"Reputation management isn't manual, it's systematically attentive."

AI FOR LOCAL LINK BUILDING & CITATIONS

Rachel owns a physical therapy practice and had been struggling to compete with larger clinics in her area. Her website was well-designed, her content was helpful, and her Google Business Profile was optimized. But she still wasn't ranking well for competitive local searches.

The missing piece was local authority, the digital signals that tell search engines other local businesses and organizations recognize and trust her practice.

When we audited Rachel's backlink profile, the problem became clear. Her website had exactly three local links: one from her professional association, one from her chamber of commerce listing, and one from a local business directory she'd submitted to years ago.

Meanwhile, her top competitor had 47 local links from neighborhood blogs, local news mentions, community event listings, healthcare directories, and partnerships with other local businesses.

Rachel wasn't getting local links because she didn't have a system for finding and earning them. That's where AI transformed her approach.

We implemented an AI-powered local link building strategy that:
- Identified 73 local websites, blogs, and organizations that regularly linked to businesses like hers
- Discovered 12 "unlinked mentions" where local sites mentioned her practice without linking
- Found 8 broken links on local websites that we could offer to replace with relevant content
- Automated personalized outreach to local bloggers and community websites
- Monitored competitor link acquisition to identify new opportunities

Within six months, Rachel's local link profile grew from 3 to 34 high-quality local links. Her local search rankings improved dramatically, she went from page 2 to position 2-4 for her main keywords. More importantly, referral traffic from local websites increased 156%, bringing in patients who were already pre qualified by trusted local sources.

That's what happens when you stop hoping for local links and start systematically earning them.

Why Local Links Matter More Than Ever

Many local businesses focus exclusively on Google Business Profile optimization and forget about traditional link building. This is a mistake that costs them significant search visibility.

Local links serve multiple purposes:

Search Engine Authority: Links from local websites signal to Google that you're a legitimate, trusted business in your community

Geographic Relevance: Links from local sources reinforce your connection to specific neighborhoods and service areas

Referral Traffic: Local websites send pre-qualified visitors who are already interested in local services

Community Connection: Being mentioned by local organizations positions you as a community member, not just a business

Competitive Advantage: Most local businesses don't actively build local links, creating opportunities for those who do
The businesses that dominate local search aren't just optimizing their own websites, they're building relationships and earning recognition throughout their local digital ecosystem.

The Five Pillars of AI-Powered Local Link Building

1. AI Discovers Relevant Local Linking Opportunities
Traditional link building often involves cold outreach to random websites. AI-powered local link building is different, it identifies websites that are already linking to businesses like yours or discussing topics relevant to your services.

AI tools can analyze:

Local news websites: Find journalists who write about your industry or local business topics

Community blogs: Identify bloggers who feature local businesses or write about relevant topics

Event websites: Discover local events where your expertise or sponsorship might be valuable

Business directories: Find industry-specific or geographic directories that provide valuable links

Local organization websites: Identify nonprofits, chambers, and associations relevant to your business

Competitor backlinks: Analyze where competitors are getting local links you could potentially earn

A financial planner used AI to discover that the local university's business school frequently featured local professionals in their newsletter. She reached out with an offer to speak at student events and earned both a valuable link and several new clients from faculty referrals.

2. Tailored Outreach Templates Ensure Personalization at Scale

Generic link building emails get ignored. Effective local outreach requires personalization that shows you understand the local community and the specific website you're contacting.

AI can help create personalized outreach by:

Analyzing website content: Understanding what topics and angles resonate with each site
Identifying mutual connections: Finding shared community ties or business relationships
Researching recent content: Referencing specific articles or posts that show you actually read their site
Customizing value propositions: Explaining how your content or expertise serves their specific audience
Timing optimization: Sending outreach when recipients are most likely to respond

A veterinarian used AI-personalized outreach to local pet bloggers, referencing their recent articles and offering to contribute expert advice. Her response rate was 34% compared to the typical 2-5% for generic outreach emails.

3. AI Citation Consistency Monitoring and Management

Citations (mentions of your business name, address, and phone number) across local directories and websites significantly impact local search rankings. But managing citations manually across hundreds of potential sites is nearly impossible.

AI can:

Monitor citation accuracy: Track your business information across 200+ directories and websites

Identify inconsistencies: Flag variations in business name, address, phone, or website that hurt search performance

Prioritize corrections: Focus on the most important directories first based on their impact on local search

Automate submissions: Submit your business to new directories that become relevant to your industry

Track competitor citations: See where competitors are listed that you're missing

A restaurant discovered through AI monitoring that their phone number was listed incorrectly on 23 local directories, sending hungry customers to a disconnected number. Fixing these citations resulted in a 28% increase in phone orders within 60 days.

4. Unlinked Mention Discovery and Conversion

Local websites and blogs often mention businesses without linking to them. These "unlinked mentions" represent easy link building opportunities since the website has already acknowledged your business.

AI tools can:

Scan local websites: Find mentions of your business name across local sites and blogs

Monitor social media: Identify social posts that mention your business without linking

Track news mentions: Discover local media coverage that doesn't include website links

Identify review mentions: Find review discussions on local forums or Facebook groups

Set up ongoing alerts: Get notified immediately when new unlinked mentions appear

A home services contractor discovered that a local news article about storm damage mentioned his company by name but didn't link to his website. A simple email to the journalist resulted in the link being added, driving 47 new visitors in the first week.

5. Link Impact Measurement and Portfolio Growth

Building local links is only valuable if those links actually improve your search rankings and bring qualified traffic. AI helps measure and optimize your link building efforts:

Link quality scoring: Evaluate the authority and relevance of potential link sources

Traffic analysis: Track referral visits and conversions from specific local links

Ranking correlation: Monitor how new local links affect your search position for target keywords

Competitor gap analysis: Identify high-value link opportunities your competitors have that you don't

ROI calculation: Measure the business impact of link building efforts to justify continued investment

The AI Local Link Building Process

Phase 1: Local Link Landscape Analysis (Week 1)

Use AI to map your local linking opportunities:
- Competitor backlink analysis: Identify where local competitors are getting quality links
- Local website discovery: Find community sites, blogs, and organizations in your area
- Industry directory research: Locate relevant business directories and professional associations
- Content opportunity assessment: Identify local websites that accept guest content or business features
- Partnership potential evaluation: Find local businesses and organizations for collaboration opportunities

Phase 2: Current Citation and Link Audit (Week 1)
Assess your existing local link profile:
- Citation inventory: Catalog all current directory listings and local mentions
- Link quality evaluation: Analyze the authority and relevance of current backlinks
- Consistency check: Identify variations in business information across different sites
- Unlinked mention discovery: Find existing mentions that could become links
- Gap identification: Compare your profile to successful local competitors

Phase 3: Outreach Campaign Development (Week 2)
Create personalized outreach strategies:
- Contact research: Find decision makers at target websites and organizations
- Value proposition development: Create compelling reasons for each site to link to you
- Content creation: Develop resources, guides, or articles that provide value to local audiences
- Email template customization: Personalize outreach for different types of opportunities
- Follow-up sequence planning: Create systematic follow-up processes for initial outreach

Phase 4: Implementation and Monitoring (Ongoing)
Execute and optimize your local link building:

- Systematic outreach: Send personalized emails to prioritized targets
- Relationship building: Engage with local websites through social media and comments
- Content promotion: Share valuable content with local influencers and organizations
- Citation management: Correct inconsistencies and submit to new relevant directories
- Performance tracking: Monitor link acquisition, rankings, and referral traffic

Types of Local Link Opportunities

Community Involvement Links

Local nonprofits: Board positions, volunteer work, or donations often result in website mentions and links
Community events: Sponsorships, speaking engagements, or participation in local events
School partnerships: Programs with local schools or educational institutions
Chamber of commerce: Membership benefits often include directory listings and event mentions
Local sports teams: Sponsorships or partnerships with community sports organizations

Content-Based Link Opportunities

Local news websites: Expert commentary, press releases, or newsworthy business updates
Community blogs: Guest posts, interviews, or collaborative content projects
Industry publications: Local trade publications or professional association content
Resource pages: Getting listed on local "recommended business" or resource directories
Local guides: Inclusion in community guides, visitor resources, or local business features
Partnership and Networking Links
Vendor relationships: Links from suppliers, partners, or service providers
Client relationships: Links from satisfied business clients (B2B services)
Professional networks: Links from colleagues, referral partners, or industry connections
Local business collaborations: Joint promotions, events, or content projects
Cross-promotional opportunities: Mutual linking with complementary local businesses

Advanced Local Link Building Strategies

The Local Expert Positioning Approach

Position yourself as the go-to expert for your industry in your area:
- Local media relationships: Regular commentary on industry trends for local news
- Community education: Free workshops or seminars that generate local coverage
- Industry trend analysis: Local perspective on national industry developments
- Crisis response: Expert guidance during industry-related local emergencies or challenges

The Community Value Strategy

Create genuine value for your local community:
- Local resource development: Comprehensive guides or tools for local residents
- Community problem solving: Address local challenges through your expertise
- Educational content: Free training or information that helps local businesses or residents
- Event organization: Host or co-host events that benefit the local community

The Broken Link Recovery Method

Find and fix broken links on local websites:
- Local website auditing: Use AI to identify broken links on local sites
- Content replacement offers: Provide updated content to replace broken link destinations
- Resource page maintenance: Help local sites keep their resource pages current and functional
- Archive link recovery: Replace links to discontinued local businesses or services

Tools for AI-Powered Local Link Building

Ahrefs or SEMrush: Comprehensive backlink analysis and competitor research
HARO (Help a Reporter Out): Connect with journalists seeking expert sources
BuzzSumo: Find local content creators and influencers in your industry
Google Alerts: Monitor mentions of your business and industry topics Pitchbox or NinjaOutreach: Automate and personalize link building outreach Moz Local or BrightLocal: Manage citations and local directory listings Mention or Brand24:

Track unlinked mentions across the web

Common Local Link Building Mistakes

The Quantity Over Quality Trap

Pursuing low-quality local directory links instead of fewer high-authority local connections.

The Generic Outreach Problem

Sending template emails that don't demonstrate knowledge of local community or specific websites.

The One-Time Campaign Error

Treating link building as a one-time project instead of ongoing relationship building.

The Citation Inconsistency Issue

Building new links while allowing existing citations to remain inaccurate or incomplete.

The Value Deficit Mistake

Asking for links without offering genuine value to the linking website or their audience.

Measuring Local Link Building Success

Track metrics that indicate real business impact:

Link Metrics:
- Number of new local links acquired monthly
- Domain authority and relevance of linking sites
- Anchor text diversity and optimization
- Geographic distribution of linking domains

Search Performance Metrics:
- Local search ranking improvements for target keywords
- Increase in local search visibility and impressions
- Map Pack inclusion frequency improvements
- Voice search ranking performance

Traffic and Conversion Metrics:

- Referral traffic from local linking sites
- Lead generation attributed to referral traffic
- Phone calls and form submissions from local links
- Revenue generated from locally-sourced website traffic

Building Your Local Link Strategy

Month 1: Complete local link landscape analysis and current profile audit Month 2: Begin systematic outreach to highest-priority local opportunities Month 3: Focus on citation consistency and unlinked mention conversion Month 4+: Scale successful tactics and explore advanced community positioning strategies

The Compound Effect of Local Links

Local link building creates compounding benefits over time:

Immediate benefits: Direct referral traffic and search ranking improvements
Medium-term benefits: Increased local brand recognition and community connections
Long-term benefits: Sustainable competitive advantages and community positioning

Your competitors are likely ignoring local link building or approaching it haphazardly. While they focus only on on-site optimization, you can build a local authority that becomes INCREASINGLY ly difficult to compete with.

The businesses that dominate local search long-term aren't just optimizing their own websites, they're building relationships and earning recognition throughout their entire local community.

AI makes this relationship building scalable and systematic. You're not just hoping for local links, you're strategically earning them from sources that matter most to your search visibility and business growth.

Remember: local link building isn't about manipulation or shortcuts. It's about systematically demonstrating your value to the local community and earning recognition from organizations and websites that your potential customers already trust

Key Insights

"Link building locally isn't cold outreach, it's community building."
"AI surfaces opportunities you'd never spot manually."
"Citations are breadcrumbs, AI keeps them consistent."
"Mentions without links are signals; AI helps you claim them."
"A link today can be a client tomorrow."

VOICE SEARCH & CONVERSATIONAL AI FOR LOCAL SUCCESS

Kevin runs a successful bakery that had been ranking well for traditional searches like "bakery downtown" and "fresh bread delivery." His website got decent traffic, and his Google Business Profile was optimized. But he noticed something troubling in his analytics: while overall local search was growing, his website traffic was plateauing.

The problem became clear when we analyzed how people were actually finding local businesses. Voice search had quietly become the dominant way people searched for local services on mobile devices. And Kevin's bakery wasn't optimized for how people actually talk when they search.

When someone types a search, they might enter "bakery gluten free options." But when they speak to their phone, they ask, "Where can I get gluten-free muffins for my daughter's school party tomorrow?"

Kevin's website was optimized for the typed search but invisible for the spoken one.

We implemented a voice search optimization strategy that transformed Kevin's approach:

- Added conversational FAQ sections that answered complete questions people ask
- Optimized content for natural language queries instead of keyword fragments
- Created "answer box" content that directly addressed common voice searches
- Implemented a chatbot that could handle voice-to-text inquiries about daily specials
- Structured all location and hours information for voice assistant compatibility

The results were immediate and dramatic. Within 90 days, Kevin's mobile traffic increased 127%. More importantly, the quality of inquiries improved, customers were calling with specific requests for items they'd heard about through voice search results.

His bakery started appearing in voice search results for queries like "where can I get birthday cake today," "best croissants near me right now," and "bakery open early Sunday morning." These conversational searches brought in customers with immediate, specific needs who were ready to buy.

That's the power of optimizing for how people actually search when they're using their voice instead of their fingers.

Why Voice Search Changes Everything for Local Businesses

Voice search isn't just a different way to type, it represents a fundamental shift in how customers find and interact with local businesses.

Voice searches are more conversational: People speak in complete sentences with context and urgency

Voice searches are more local: 58% of voice searches are for local business information

Voice searches indicate immediate intent: People use voice when they need something now, not later

Voice searches are longer: Average voice search is 4-7 words vs. 2-3 words for typed searches

Voice searches expect direct answers: Users want immediate, specific responses to their questions

Traditional SEO optimizes for how people type. Voice search optimization addresses how people actually talk, and there's a big difference.

Typed search: "Italian restaurant downtown" Voice search: "What's the best Italian restaurant open for dinner tonight?"

Typed search: "emergency dentist" Voice search: "I have a terrible toothache, who can see me today?"

Typed search: "auto repair brake service" Voice search: "My brakes are making a grinding noise, where can I get them fixed?"

The businesses that optimize for voice search capture customers at the moment of need with specific, actionable solutions.

The Five Pillars of Voice Search Optimization for Local Business

1. Natural Language Content Structure

Voice search optimization requires content that matches how people actually speak, not how they type keywords into search boxes.

This means creating content that:

Answers complete questions: Instead of targeting "plumbing repair costs," create content that answers "How much does it cost to fix a leaky pipe?"

Uses conversational language: Write as if you're speaking to a friend, not writing a technical manual

Includes location context: "If you live in the downtown area..." instead of just "downtown plumbing services"

Addresses urgency: Voice searchers often need immediate solutions

Provides specific, actionable answers: Voice search users want direct answers, not pages of information to sort through

A veterinary clinic rewrote their emergency services page to answer voice searches like "my dog ate chocolate what should I do" and "where can I take my cat tonight for emergency care." Their emergency appointment bookings increased 78% as they started capturing voice searches from worried pet owners.

2. AI Predicts Conversational Local Questions

AI analysis can reveal the actual questions people ask about your business and services, not just the keywords they type.

AI tools can analyze:

"People Also Ask" data: Google's suggestions for related questions
Voice search query logs: Actual spoken searches in your industry and location
Customer service transcripts: Questions people ask when they call your business
Social media conversations: How people discuss problems and solutions online
Review analysis: Questions and concerns mentioned in customer feedback

A home security company used AI to discover that most voice searches weren't for "home security systems" but for questions like "how do I keep my house safe while I'm traveling" and "what should I do if my alarm keeps going off." They created FAQ content addressing these specific concerns and saw a 156% increase in consultation requests from mobile traffic.

3. Chatbots Provide Instant Voice-Compatible Responses

Voice search often leads to immediate follow-up questions. A chatbot powered by local business knowledge can provide instant responses that keep potential customers engaged instead of leaving to find answers elsewhere.

Effective local business chatbots can:

Answer basic service questions: Hours, pricing, availability, and location information
Schedule appointments: Integration with calendar systems for immediate booking
Provide detailed directions: Step-by-step guidance including parking and entrance information
Handle emergency inquiries: Triage urgent requests and connect customers with appropriate staff
Offer personalized recommendations: Suggest services based on customer needs and location

A dental practice implemented a chatbot that could answer voice-initiated questions about emergency appointments, insurance acceptance, and available appointment times. The chatbot handled 67% of after-hours inquiries automatically, converted 23% of interactions to appointment bookings, and reduced staff time spent on routine questions by 89%.

4. Voice-Optimized FAQ Development

The key to voice search success is anticipating and answering the complete questions your customers ask, not just optimizing for keyword fragments.
Voice-optimized FAQs should:

Address specific customer situations: "What should I do if my air conditioner stops working on a weekend?"
Include location and timing context: "Do you provide same-day service in the northern suburbs?"

Answer follow-up questions: Provide comprehensive responses that address likely next questions

Use natural, conversational language: Write as if you're speaking directly to the customer
Include clear calls-to-action: Make the next step obvious for voice search users

An accounting firm created voice-optimized FAQs that answered questions like "what documents do I need for my tax appointment," "how much does tax preparation cost for a small business," and "can you help me if I haven't filed taxes in three years." These conversational answers started appearing in voice search results and increased new client consultations by 43%.

5. Voice Search Performance Measurement

Success in voice search requires different metrics than traditional SEO because voice search behavior and outcomes differ from typed searches.

Key voice search metrics include:

Featured snippet appearances: Voice assistants often read featured snippet content for answers
Mobile click-to-call rates: Voice searchers frequently call businesses immediately
Direct traffic increases: Voice search often leads to brand searches and direct website visits
Local action completion: Voice search users complete local actions (visits, calls, appointments) at higher rates
Query satisfaction rates: Bounce rates and time on site for voice-initiated traffic

The Voice Search Optimization Process

Phase 1: Voice Search Audit and Opportunity Assessment (Week 1)

Analyze your current voice search performance:

- Current voice search visibility: Check if your content appears in voice search results
- Competitor voice search analysis: See which competitors rank for conversational queries
- Question research: Identify the actual questions customers ask about your services
- Content gap analysis: Find voice search opportunities your current content doesn't address
- Technical voice search requirements: Assess site speed, mobile optimization, and structured data

Phase 2: Conversational Content Development (Week 2-3)

Create content optimized for natural language queries:

- FAQ page expansion: Develop comprehensive answers to voice-likely questions
- Question-based blog posts: Write content that directly answers common voice searches
- Location-specific voice content: Create content for neighborhood-specific voice queries
- Service-specific conversational pages: Optimize service pages for how people talk about problems
- Emergency and urgent need content: Address immediate-need voice searches

Phase 3: Technical Voice Search Implementation (Week 3)

Optimize technical elements for voice search compatibility:

- Structured data markup: Implement schema that helps voice assistants understand your content
- Site speed optimization: Voice search users expect instant loading times
- Mobile experience improvement: Voice searches are predominantly mobile
- Local business markup: Ensure location, hours, and contact information are voice-accessible
- Answer box optimization: Format content to capture featured snippets that voice assistants read

Phase 4: Voice Search Monitoring and Optimization (Ongoing)

Track voice search performance and continuously improve:
- Voice search ranking monitoring: Track positions for conversational queries
- Mobile traffic analysis: Monitor mobile traffic patterns and user behavior
- Call tracking: Measure phone calls generated from voice search traffic
- Featured snippet tracking: Monitor featured snippet appearances for target questions
- User experience optimization: Improve based on voice search user behavior data

Voice Search Content Strategies That Work

The Complete Answer Approach
Voice search users want complete, actionable answers, not partial information that requires additional research.

Instead of: "We provide brake repair services" Try: "If your brakes are making grinding noises, squealing, or taking longer to stop your car, you likely need brake repair. We can diagnose brake problems and complete most repairs the same day. Call us at [number] to schedule an inspection, or visit our shop at [address] Monday through Saturday 8 AM to 6 PM."

The Local Context Strategy

Include location-specific information that makes your answers more relevant for local voice searches.

Instead of: "Our restaurant serves authentic Italian cuisine" Try: "Located in the heart of downtown on Main Street, our family-owned Italian restaurant has been serving authentic pasta, wood-fired pizza, and traditional Italian desserts to local families since 1987. We're open for lunch and dinner Tuesday through Sunday, with outdoor seating available and parking available in the municipal lot behind our building."

The Problem-Solution Framework

Structure content to address the complete customer journey from problem recognition to solution.

Problem identification: "If you're experiencing [specific symptoms]..." Immediate action: "Here's what you should do right now..." Professional solution: "For a permanent fix, you'll need..." How to contact you: "We can help you with..." Next steps: "To schedule service, call or visit..."

Voice Search and Local Business Types

Service-Based Businesses

Voice search is particularly valuable for service businesses because customers often search for immediate solutions:

- "My toilet is overflowing, who can help me now?"
- "I locked my keys in my car downtown, who can unlock it?"
- "My dog needs to see a vet today, who's open?"
- "I need someone to fix my garage door this weekend"

Retail and Restaurant Businesses

Voice search helps capture customers with immediate purchase intent:

- "Where can I buy fresh flowers for a dinner party tonight?"
- "What restaurant near me serves good vegetarian food?"
- "Do any stores around here sell organic dog food?"
- "Where can I get birthday cake this afternoon?"

Professional Services

Voice search often precedes scheduled appointments and consultations:

- "I need to find a good accountant for my small business"
- "Who can help me with my divorce in [city]?"
- "I need to see a dermatologist about this rash"
- "Where can I get help with my tax problems?"

Common Voice Search Optimization Mistakes

The Keyword Stuffing Problem

Forcing traditional keywords into conversational content instead of writing naturally.

The Incomplete Answer Issue
Providing partial information that forces voice search users to search again elsewhere.

The Technical Neglect Error
Focusing only on content without optimizing technical elements like site speed and mobile experience.

The Question Assumption Mistake
Assuming you know what questions customers ask instead of researching actual voice search queries.

The Desktop-First Trap
Optimizing for desktop experience when voice search is predominantly mobile.

Tools for Voice Search Optimization

AnswerThePublic: Discover question-based searches related to your business

SEMrush or Ahrefs: Track voice search keyword opportunities and featured snippets

Google Search Console: Monitor mobile traffic and query performance

Schema.org markup tools: Implement structured data for voice search compatibility

Google's Mobile-Friendly Test: Ensure mobile optimization for voice search users

PageSpeed Insights: Optimize loading speed for immediate voice search expectations

The Future of Local Voice Search

Voice search adoption continues accelerating, especially for local business queries:
- Smart speaker growth: More households have voice-activated devices
- Mobile voice search: Smartphone voice search usage increases annually
- Car integration: Voice search in vehicles for local business discovery
- Improved accuracy: Voice recognition technology becomes more reliable
- Multilingual capabilities: Voice search expands to serve diverse local communities

The businesses that optimize for voice search now will have sustainable advantages as adoption continues growing.

Building Your Voice Search Strategy

Month 1: Complete voice search audit and develop FAQ content strategy Month 2: Implement technical optimizations and create conversational content Month 3: Launch chatbot integration and monitor voice search performance Month 4+: Refine based on performance data and expand voice search content

Your Voice Search Competitive Advantage

While most local businesses still optimize only for typed searches, voice search represents a massive opportunity to capture customers with immediate, specific needs.

Your competitors are optimizing for "restaurant downtown." You can optimize for "where can I get a good dinner tonight that's not too expensive and has parking."

They're targeting "auto repair." You can capture "my check engine light just came on, where should I take my car."

Voice search users aren't just browsing, they're actively seeking solutions. When your business provides the complete, conversational answer they're looking for, you don't just get a website visitor. You get a customer who's ready to take action.

The businesses that master voice search optimization won't just rank better, they'll connect with customers at the exact moment when they need what you provide.

Key Insights

"Your customers don't search with pages, they ask questions."
"Answer the question they'll speak, not just the one they'll type."
"A friendly local chatbot is better than a silent website."
"Voice SEO is about connection, not just keywords."
"Be the answer, not just another search result."

AI ANALYTICS: MEASURING LOCAL VISIBILITY & GROWTH

James runs a roofing company that had implemented everything we'd discussed in the previous chapters. His website was optimized, his Google Business Profile was active, he was getting reviews consistently, and his content targeted voice search. But he was frustrated because he couldn't tell which efforts were actually driving business.

"I'm doing all this digital marketing," he told me, "but I still don't know if it's working. I get calls, but I don't know where they're coming from. I see my website traffic going up, but I can't connect it to actual jobs."

James had the classic local business analytics problem: lots of activity but no clear understanding of what was driving results.

That's when we implemented an AI-powered analytics dashboard that changed everything.

Instead of looking at generic website metrics, James could now see:
- Which neighborhoods were driving the most qualified leads
- What specific keywords were generating calls versus just website visits
- How weather patterns affected search demand for emergency roofing services
- Which content pieces led to the highest-value customer inquiries
- The complete customer journey from initial search to signed contract

The insights were immediately actionable. AI analysis revealed that customers who found James through searches related to "storm damage" were 340% more likely to hire his company than those who found him through general "roofing contractor" searches. It showed that leads from certain neighborhoods had an average project value 67% higher than others.

Most importantly, the AI dashboard could predict demand. When weather forecasts showed potential storm activity, James could see search volume spiking 2-3 days before the weather hit. This allowed him to adjust his advertising spend, prepare his team, and capture more emergency service opportunities.

Within six months, James increased his revenue 156% not by working more, but by focusing his efforts on the activities and areas that the data showed generated the best customers.

That's what happens when you stop guessing about your marketing performance and start measuring what actually drives business growth.

Why Traditional Analytics Fail Local Businesses

Most local businesses rely on basic website analytics that tell them how many people visited their site but not whether those visits turned into customers. This creates a dangerous illusion of progress without actual business results.

Traditional analytics problems for local businesses:

Generic metrics don't indicate local performance: Total website traffic means nothing if it's not from your service area
No connection between online activity and offline results: Website visits don't automatically translate to phone calls or in-person visits
Lack of geographic segmentation: You can't optimize local marketing if you don't know which areas perform best
Missing attribution: Multiple touchpoints before customers contact you make it hard to credit the right marketing efforts
Reactive rather than predictive: Historical data doesn't help you anticipate and prepare for demand changes

AI-powered local analytics solve these problems by connecting online activity to actual business outcomes and providing predictive insights that help you stay ahead of demand.

The Five Pillars of AI-Powered Local Analytics

1. Neighborhood-Level Performance Analysis

AI can segment your performance data by geographic areas much smaller than cities or zip codes, revealing which neighborhoods, streets, or even building complexes generate the best customers.
This geographic analysis reveals:

High-value customer concentration: Specific areas where customers spend more on average
Service demand patterns: Neighborhoods where certain services are more popular
Seasonal variations by area: How different locations show different seasonal patterns
Competition intensity: Areas where you're winning versus losing to competitors
Growth opportunities: Underserved areas where you could expand effectively

A landscaping company discovered through AI geographic analysis that customers in one specific neighborhood consistently hired them for full landscape redesigns averaging $12,000, while customers from other areas typically requested $800 maintenance services. They adjusted their marketing to focus more resources on the high-value neighborhood and increased their average project value by 89%.

2. Multi-Channel Attribution That Actually Works

Local customers don't follow linear paths from search to purchase. They might find you on Google, check your reviews on Facebook, visit your website, drive by your location, and then call three weeks later.

AI attribution analysis can:
Track customer touchpoints across channels: Connect online research to offline conversions
Identify influential touchpoints: Determine which interactions most impact customer decisions
Measure cumulative campaign effects: See how multiple marketing efforts work together
Calculate true ROI: Attribute revenue to the marketing activities that actually generated it
Optimize budget allocation: Shift spending to channels and tactics that drive best results

A dental practice discovered that patients who engaged with their educational blog content before booking appointments had a 78% higher lifetime value than those who booked immediately after a Google Ad click. They shifted budget from direct advertising to content marketing and increased patient value while reducing acquisition costs.

3. Predictive Local Demand Forecasting

AI can analyze historical patterns, seasonal trends, weather data, local events, and economic indicators to predict when demand for your services will spike or decline.

Predictive insights include:
Seasonal demand patterns: When different services peak throughout the year
Weather-related opportunities: How weather conditions drive demand for specific services Local event impacts: How community events, construction projects, or economic changes affect business
Competitor activity effects: How competitor actions impact your market share
Economic trend correlations: How local economic indicators predict service demand
An HVAC company used AI demand forecasting to predict air conditioning repair calls based on weather forecasts. When temperatures were projected to exceed 85°F for three consecutive days, their emergency service calls typically increased 234%. They began scheduling extra technicians and ordering parts in advance, reducing response times and capturing more market share during peak demand periods.

4. Content Performance and Keyword Success Measurement

AI can connect content performance directly to business results, showing which blog posts, pages, and keywords generate leads versus which only generate traffic
Content intelligence includes:

Lead-generating content identification: Which pages convert visitors to customers most effectively
Keyword value analysis: Which search terms bring customers who actually hire you
Content journey mapping: How customers move through your content before converting
Topic performance trends: Which subjects resonate most with your target audience
Competitor content gaps: Opportunities where competitors aren't serving customer information needs

A financial planner discovered that visitors who read her "retirement planning for teachers" article were 456% more likely to schedule consultations than visitors who read general investment content. She created more profession-specific content and saw consultation bookings increase 67% while reducing overall content production time.

5. Real-Time Business Intelligence and Alerts

AI monitoring can alert you to opportunities and problems as they develop, allowing you to respond quickly rather than discovering issues weeks later in monthly reports.

Real-time intelligence includes:

Demand spike alerts: Immediate notification when search volume increases for your services
Reputation monitoring: Instant alerts when reviews or mentions require attention
Competitor activity tracking: Notifications when competitors change tactics or pricing
Technical issue detection: Immediate alerts for website problems that could cost you leads
Opportunity identification: Real-time discovery of trending local topics you could address

A plumbing company received AI alerts showing search volume for "burst pipe repair" spiking during a cold snap. They immediately increased their Google Ads budget for emergency keywords and deployed additional technicians. They captured 34% more emergency service calls than during previous similar weather events.

The AI Local Analytics Implementation Process

Phase 1: Analytics Audit and Goal Definition (Week 1)

Assess your current analytics setup and define success metrics:
- Current analytics review: Evaluate existing tracking and identify gaps
- Business goal alignment: Connect analytics metrics to actual business objectives
- Customer journey mapping: Understand how customers find and choose your business
- Key performance indicator selection: Choose metrics that indicate real business success
- Benchmark establishment: Set baseline measurements for improvement tracking

Phase 2: Advanced Tracking Implementation (Week 2)

Set up comprehensive tracking that connects online activity to business outcomes:
- Call tracking setup: Assign unique phone numbers to different marketing channels
- Form tracking enhancement: Monitor which forms generate the highest-value leads
- Geographic segmentation: Configure analytics to report performance by service area
- Multi-channel attribution: Connect customer interactions across different touchpoints
- Conversion goal configuration: Track actions that indicate business success, not just website engagement

Phase 3: AI Dashboard Development (Week 3)

Create intelligent reporting that provides actionable insights:
- Automated reporting setup: Regular reports that highlight important trends and opportunities
- Predictive modeling implementation: Forecasting tools that anticipate demand changes
- Competitor monitoring integration: Automated tracking of competitor performance and tactics
- Real-time alert configuration: Immediate notifications for opportunities and problems
- Mobile dashboard access: Analytics accessible from anywhere for quick decision-making

Phase 4: Optimization and Refinement (Ongoing)

Use AI insights to continuously improve marketing performance:
- Performance analysis: Regular review of what's working and what isn't
- Strategy adjustments: Modify tactics based on data-driven insights
- Budget optimization: Shift resources to highest-performing activities and areas
- Content strategy refinement: Create more content similar to top-performing pieces
- Expansion opportunity identification: Find new markets or services based on demand data

Key Local Business Metrics That Matter

Revenue-Connected Metrics

Customer Acquisition Cost by Channel: How much you spend to acquire customers from different marketing sources
Customer Lifetime Value by Source: Which marketing channels bring customers who spend the most over time

Revenue per Lead by Geographic Area: Which neighborhoods or areas generate the highest-value customers
Conversion Rate by Service Type: Which services have the highest inquiry-to-sale conversion rates

Operational Intelligence Metrics

Response Time Impact: How quickly answering calls or emails affects conversion rates
Seasonal Demand Patterns: Monthly and weekly patterns that help with staff and inventory planning
Service Area Performance: Geographic analysis of where your marketing is most effective
Competitive Share of Voice: How your online presence compares to competitors in key searches

Predictive Performance Indicators

Lead Quality Trending: Whether incoming leads are getting better or worse over time
Market Demand Forecasting: Predicted demand for your services based on multiple data sources

Churn Risk Identification: Early warning signs that customers might choose competitors Growth Opportunity Scoring: Data-driven identification of expansion opportunities

Tools for AI-Powered Local Analytics

Comprehensive Analytics Platforms

Google Analytics 4: Advanced attribution and predictive capabilities for local businesses
HubSpot: Integrated analytics that connect marketing activities to revenue outcomes
Salesforce Analytics: Enterprise-level insights connecting all customer touchpoints
CallRail: Call tracking and conversation analytics specifically for local businesses
Specialized Local Business Tools
BirdEye: Reputation management with predictive analytics for review and customer sentiment
ReviewTrackers: AI-powered review analysis and sentiment tracking
BrightLocal: Local SEO tracking with geographic performance analysis
LocalClarity: Google Business Profile analytics with competitive intelligence

Predictive and AI Tools

Google Trends: Identify seasonal patterns and emerging demand for your services
SEMrush or Ahrefs: Competitor analysis and keyword performance tracking
Tableau or Power BI: Advanced data visualization for complex local market analysis
DataStudio: Custom dashboard creation connecting multiple data sources

Common Local Analytics Mistakes

The Vanity Metrics Trap

Focusing on impressive-sounding numbers like total website traffic instead of metrics that indicate business success.

The Attribution Oversimplification Error

Crediting conversions to the last interaction instead of understanding the complete customer journey.

The Geographic Blindness Problem

Analyzing performance at city or state level instead of neighborhood-specific insights that drive local marketing decisions.

The Reactive-Only Approach

Using analytics only to understand what happened instead of predicting what's coming next.

The Tool Overload Issue

Implementing multiple analytics tools without connecting them to create comprehensive business intelligence.

Building Your Local Analytics Strategy

Month 1: Foundation Setup
- Implement comprehensive tracking across all marketing channels
- Configure geographic and demographic segmentation
- Establish baseline performance measurements
- Set up basic automated reporting

Month 2: Advanced Intelligence
- Deploy predictive analytics for demand forecasting
- Implement competitor monitoring and benchmarking
- Create real-time alert systems for opportunities and issues
- Develop custom dashboards for key business metrics

Month 3: Optimization and Scaling
- Use data insights to optimize marketing budget allocation
- Refine targeting based on high-performing geographic and demographic segments
- Expand successful tactics to new markets or services
- Develop advanced predictive models for business planning

Month 4+: Strategic Intelligence
- Build comprehensive customer journey analysis
- Implement advanced attribution modeling
- Create predictive customer lifetime value models
- Develop data-driven expansion and investment strategies

Making Analytics Actionable for Local Businesses
The goal of AI analytics isn't just to have better data, it's to make better decisions that grow your business.

Weekly Action Items: Use analytics to identify immediate opportunities and problems requiring attention
Monthly Strategy Reviews: Analyze trends and patterns to adjust marketing tactics and budget allocation
Quarterly Planning: Use predictive insights to plan for seasonal changes and market opportunities
Annual Strategy Development: Leverage comprehensive data analysis for major business planning and investment decisions

Your Analytics Competitive Advantage

While most local businesses rely on gut feelings and basic website stats, AI-powered analytics give you the intelligence to:
- Know exactly which marketing activities generate the best customers
- Predict demand changes before competitors see them
- Focus resources on highest-value opportunities
- Respond to market changes faster than competition
- Make expansion decisions based on data rather than guesswork

Your competitors are optimizing blindly. You're optimizing with precision. They're reacting to market changes. You're anticipating them.

They're spending marketing budgets on hope. You're investing based on proven performance data.

The local businesses that dominate their markets don't just work harder, they work smarter by using AI analytics to understand exactly what drives growth and focusing their efforts accordingly.

Key Insights

"What gets measured gets managed, and AI measures everything that matters."
"Local performance isn't city-wide, it's street by street."
"Today's signals tell you where to optimize tomorrow."
"Analytics without clarity is noise, AI brings clarity."
"Your dashboard is your competitive advantage."

AI-DRIVEN PAID AND ORGANIC SYNERGY

Lisa owns a successful physical therapy practice that had been running Google Ads for two years with decent results. She was getting leads, but her cost per acquisition was creeping up, and she felt like she was fighting harder for the same results.

Meanwhile, her SEO efforts were slowly improving, she was ranking better for some local searches, but progress felt painfully slow.

Lisa was treating paid ads and SEO as separate strategies, managed by different people, with different goals. That's a mistake most local businesses make.

When we analyzed Lisa's complete digital marketing picture, the opportunity became clear. Her Google Ads data revealed exactly what local searches converted best, but she wasn't creating SEO content around those high-converting keywords. Her SEO efforts were building awareness for terms that her paid ads data showed didn't convert to patients.

We implemented an AI-powered integrated strategy that transformed both her paid and organic performance:
- Used AI to identify keywords that converted well in ads but where she had poor organic rankings
- Created content targeting high-converting paid search queries to improve organic visibility
- Adjusted paid advertising to support organic rankings in competitive areas
- Coordinated messaging between paid ads and organic content for consistent brand experience
- Used organic traffic data to identify new paid advertising opportunities with lower competition

The results were dramatic. Within four months, Lisa's overall cost per acquisition decreased 43% as organic traffic began capturing searches she'd been paying for. Her organic traffic increased 127% by focusing on keywords proven to convert through paid data. Most importantly, her total leads increased 89% while her marketing costs stayed flat.

The key insight: paid advertising and SEO aren't competing strategies, they're complementary tools that work better together than either works alone.

Why Local Businesses Need Integrated Paid and Organic Strategy

Most local businesses approach digital marketing in silos. They run Google Ads managed by one person or agency, while their SEO is handled separately by someone else. This creates missed opportunities and inefficient spending.

Common problems with siloed approaches:

Duplicate efforts: Paying for ads on keywords you already rank well for organically
Missed opportunities: Not creating content for keywords that convert well in paid campaigns
Inconsistent messaging: Different value propositions in ads versus organic content
Budget inefficiency: Overspending on paid ads for searches you could capture organically
Limited data sharing: Insights from one channel don't inform strategy for the other

AI-powered integration solves these problems by analyzing performance across all channels and identifying opportunities where paid and organic efforts can amplify each other.

The Five Pillars of AI-Driven Paid and Organic Synergy

1. AI Identifies Where Paid Ads Can Support SEO Gaps

Your paid advertising data contains valuable intelligence about what local customers actually search for and which searches convert to business. AI can analyze this data to inform your organic content strategy.

AI gap analysis reveals:

High-converting keywords with poor organic rankings: Searches that generate customers through ads but where you're invisible organically
Seasonal opportunities: Times when paid ads should increase to support weak organic performance
Local search variations: Neighborhood-specific terms that convert well in ads but aren't targeted organically

Question-based searches: Voice search queries that convert in ads but lack corresponding FAQ content Service-specific gaps: Specialized services that perform well in paid but lack organic content support

A home services contractor discovered through AI analysis that "emergency plumbing weekend" generated high-value customers through ads but his website had no content targeting weekend emergency searches. He created dedicated weekend service content and saw organic traffic for emergency searches increase 156% while reducing his weekend advertising costs by 34%.

2. Geo-Targeted Ad Copy Mirrors AI-Optimized Organic Content

Consistent messaging across paid and organic channels builds trust and recognition. AI can ensure your ad copy and organic content work together to reinforce the same value propositions and local connections.

Integrated messaging strategies include:

Location-specific value propositions: Ads and content that reference the same local benefits and community connections
Service description consistency: Identical language for describing services across paid and organic content
Seasonal message coordination: Aligned timing for seasonal offers and content topics
Problem-solution matching: Ad copy that leads to organic content addressing the same customer problems
Trust signal amplification: Reviews, credentials, and social proof referenced in both paid and organic content

A dental practice used AI to align their "gentle dentistry for anxious patients" message across Google Ads and their website content. Patients who clicked ads found consistent messaging on landing pages, resulting in 67% higher conversion rates and 23% lower cost per patient acquisition.

3. Smart Bid Strategies Informed by Local Demand Intelligence

AI can analyze local demand patterns, competitor activity, and seasonal trends to optimize both paid bidding strategies and organic content timing for maximum impact.
Intelligent bidding includes:

Seasonal bid adjustments: INCREASINGLY paid spend when organic rankings are seasonally weak
Geographic bid optimization: Higher bids for areas where organic visibility is limited
Competitor response bidding: Adjusting bids based on competitor organic and paid activity
Time-of-day optimization: Coordinating paid ads with when organic content gets most engagement
Device-specific strategies: Different approaches for mobile versus desktop based on organic performance

An accounting firm used AI to discover that tax-related searches spiked every Sunday evening as people planned their week. They increased Google Ads bids for Sunday evenings while scheduling tax tip content to publish on Sunday afternoons, capturing customers in both paid and organic channels during peak intent moments.

4. Unified Customer Journey Intelligence

AI can track how customers move between paid and organic touchpoints, revealing the complete path from initial awareness to final conversion. This intelligence informs both advertising and content strategy.

Customer journey insights include:

Multi-touchpoint attribution: Understanding how paid ads and organic content work together in the conversion process
Content consumption patterns: Which organic content pieces are most effective at converting ad clickers
Retargeting opportunities: Using organic content engagement to inform paid advertising retargeting
Email integration: Coordinating paid ads with email marketing based on organic content engagement
Social proof integration: Using review and testimonial content to support both paid and organic conversion

A veterinary clinic discovered that customers who engaged with their pet care blog content after clicking ads were 234% more likely to schedule appointments. They created retargeting campaigns specifically for blog readers and saw appointment bookings increase 78% while reducing acquisition costs.

5. Shared Performance Measurement and Budget Optimization

AI can measure the combined impact of paid and organic efforts, showing how they work together to drive business results rather than competing for credit.

Integrated measurement includes:

Cross-channel attribution: Crediting conversions to the combination of touchpoints that actually influenced decisions
Lifetime value analysis: Understanding which mix of paid and organic acquisition drives highest customer value
Market share calculation: Total visibility across both paid and organic search results
Competitive analysis: How your combined paid and organic presence compares to competitors
ROI optimization: Budget allocation between paid and organic based on combined performance

The AI Paid-Organic Integration Process

Phase 1: Cross-Channel Performance Audit (Week 1)

Analyze how your current paid and organic efforts are working together or against each other:
- Keyword overlap analysis: Identify where you're paying for searches you already rank for organically
- Message consistency review: Compare value propositions across paid ads and organic content
- Customer journey mapping: Track how customers move between paid and organic touchpoints
- Budget efficiency assessment: Calculate waste from competing with yourself across channels
- Competitive gap analysis: See where competitors are stronger in combined paid and organic presence

Phase 2: Integrated Strategy Development (Week 2)

Create coordinated approaches that amplify both paid and organic performance:
- Keyword strategy alignment: Use paid conversion data to prioritize organic content creation
- Message coordination: Ensure consistent value propositions across all customer touchpoints
- Content calendar integration: Coordinate organic content publication with paid campaign timing
- Landing page optimization: Create dedicated pages that serve both paid ads and organic search
- Local targeting synchronization: Align geographic targeting across paid and organic efforts

Phase 3: AI-Powered Implementation (Week 3-4)
Deploy intelligent systems that optimize both channels simultaneously:
- Automated bid adjustments: AI bidding that considers organic ranking performance
- Content recommendation engines: AI suggestions for organic content based on paid performance data
- Cross-channel retargeting: Coordinated remarketing that leverages both paid and organic engagement
- Performance monitoring integration: Unified dashboards showing combined channel performance
- Alert systems: Notifications when changes in one channel affect the other

Phase 4: Optimization and Scaling (Ongoing)
Use AI insights to continuously improve integrated performance:
- Budget reallocation: Shift spending between channels based on combined ROI analysis
- Seasonal strategy adjustments: Modify paid and organic emphasis based on demand patterns
- New opportunity identification: Find gaps where integrated approaches could capture more market share
- Competitive response: Adjust strategies when competitors change their paid or organic tactics
- Expansion planning: Use successful integration tactics to enter new markets or services

Paid and Organic Integration Strategies by Business Type

Service-Based Local Businesses

Emergency Services: Use paid ads to capture immediate need while building organic authority for planning-stage searches

Professional Services: Paid ads for comparison shopping, organic content for education and trust building

Home Services: Coordinate seasonal paid campaigns with evergreen organic content for year-round visibility

Retail and E-commerce

Product-focused businesses: Paid ads for specific products, organic content for category education and brand building
Seasonal retailers: Heavy paid advertising during peak seasons, organic content for off-season engagement
Local stores: Paid ads for immediate promotions, organic content for community connection and loyalty

Restaurants and Hospitality

Event-driven businesses: Paid ads for immediate bookings, organic content for ongoing brand awareness
Daily service businesses: Coordinate daily specials in paid ads with menu information in organic content
Seasonal operations: Paid advertising during operating season, organic content year-round for planning

Advanced Integration Techniques

The SEO-Informed PPC Strategy

Use organic search data to optimize paid advertising:
- Long-tail organic winners: Create paid ads for organic keywords that convert but have low volume
- Seasonal organic dips: Increase paid spend when organic rankings seasonally decline
- Competitor organic gaps: Target paid ads where competitors are weak organically
- Voice search translation: Use organic voice search insights to create conversational ad copy

The PPC-Informed SEO Strategy

Use paid advertising data to guide organic content creation:
- High-converting ad keywords: Create comprehensive organic content for paid terms that convert well
- Negative keyword insights: Avoid creating content for terms that don't convert in paid campaigns
- Ad copy testing: Use successful ad headlines and descriptions to inform organic meta tags and content
- Geographic performance: Focus organic content on locations that convert well in paid campaigns

The Unified Brand Experience

Ensure customers get consistent messaging regardless of how they find you:

- Visual consistency: Same branding elements in ads and organic search results
- Message alignment: Identical value propositions across all touchpoints
- Offer coordination: Consistent promotions and pricing across paid and organic channels
- Social proof integration: Same testimonials and reviews featured in ads and organic content

Common Paid-Organic Integration Mistakes

The Cannibalization Problem

Paying for ads on keywords where you already rank #1 organically without strategic reason.

The Message Disconnect Issue

Different value propositions in paid ads versus organic content, confusing customers about what you offer.

The Budget Competition Error

Internal competition between paid and organic budgets instead of viewing them as complementary investments.

The Attribution Oversimplification Mistake

Crediting conversions to last-click instead of understanding how paid and organic work together in customer journeys.

The Tool Isolation Problem

Using separate tools for paid and organic that don't share data or insights between channels.

Measuring Integrated Success

Combined Performance Metrics

Total Search Visibility: Combined share of voice across paid and organic search results

Blended Cost Per Acquisition: Total marketing cost divided by all customers acquired through search

Market Dominance Score: Percentage of relevant searches where you appear in either paid or organic results

Customer Lifetime Value by Source Mix: How different combinations of paid and organic touchpoints affect customer value

Channel Synergy Indicators

Cross-Channel Conversion Rates: How often paid ad clickers convert through organic touchpoints (and vice versa)

Message Consistency Scores: Customer recognition and response to consistent messaging across channels

Budget Efficiency Ratios: Cost savings from reducing duplicate targeting between paid and organic

Competitive Advantage Metrics: How integrated approach affects competitive positioning

Building Your Integrated Strategy

Month 1: Foundation and Analysis
- Audit current paid and organic performance for overlap and gaps
- Implement cross-channel tracking and attribution
- Align messaging and value propositions across channels
- Identify immediate optimization opportunities

Month 2: Strategic Integration
- Develop coordinated keyword and content strategies
- Launch integrated campaigns with consistent messaging
- Implement AI tools for cross-channel optimization
- Begin testing different paid-organic combinations

Month 3: Optimization and Scaling
- Analyze integrated performance and adjust strategies
- Scale successful integrated tactics to new keywords and markets
- Implement advanced attribution and measurement systems
- Develop predictive models for budget allocation

Month 4+: Advanced Intelligence
- Use AI insights for sophisticated channel coordination
- Develop customer journey optimization across all touchpoints
- Implement automated bid and content adjustments based on integrated performance
- Expand successful integration strategies to new business areas

Your Integrated Competitive Advantage

While most local businesses treat paid advertising and SEO as separate efforts, integrated strategies create advantages that are difficult for competitors to match:

Dominant search presence: Appearing in both paid and organic results for important searches Consistent customer experience: Seamless messaging from initial ad click through organic content consumption

Data-driven optimization: Using insights from both channels to improve overall performance

Budget efficiency: Eliminating waste while maximizing total search visibility

Competitive resilience: Multiple ways to maintain visibility even when one channel faces challenges

Your competitors are optimizing channels in isolation. You're optimizing for total customer experience and maximum business impact.

The businesses that master AI-driven paid and organic integration don't just get better results from each channel, they create synergies that multiply the effectiveness of their entire digital marketing investment.

Key Insights

"SEO and paid ads aren't rivals, they're teammates."
"If search is local, your ads should feel local too."
"AI lets your ads mirror the search intent you're ranking for."
"Spend smarter when you know where demand lives."
"When organic drives awareness, ads capture demand."

SCALING ACROSS MULTIPLE LOCAL MARKETS

Carlos built a successful auto repair shop that dominated local search in his city. His Google Business Profile was optimized, his review acquisition system was generating steady positive feedback, and his voice search optimization was capturing mobile customers. But Carlos had bigger ambitions.

He wanted to expand to three neighboring cities, each about 30-45 minutes from his original location. The traditional approach would have meant starting over in each market, building local citations, earning reviews, creating location-specific content, and establishing credibility from scratch.

That approach would have taken years and cost thousands in duplicated effort. Instead, we implemented an AI-powered multi-market expansion strategy that transformed Carlos's approach to scaling local presence.

Rather than starting from zero in each new market, AI helped us:
- Analyze successful strategies from his original location and adapt them for each new market
- Create location-specific content variations that maintained quality while avoiding duplicate content penalties
- Identify unique opportunities and challenges in each target market before expansion
- Automate citation building and review management across all locations simultaneously
- Develop market-specific advertising strategies based on local competition and demand patterns

Within eight months, Carlos had established strong local presence in all three new markets. More importantly, his expansion was profitable from month three in each location because AI helped him avoid the typical mistakes and inefficiencies of geographic expansion.

His original location continued growing while the new markets generated an additional $180,000 in annual revenue. The systematic, AI-powered approach meant each new market reached profitability 67% faster than his original location had.

That's what happens when you scale local marketing strategically instead of starting over in each new market.

Why Most Local Business Expansion Fails

The majority of local businesses that attempt geographic expansion struggle because they treat each new market like a completely separate business. This creates enormous inefficiencies and often leads to failed expansion attempts.

Common expansion mistakes:

Starting from scratch mentality: Ignoring lessons learned and proven strategies from existing locations
Generic template approach: Using identical content and strategies without local market adaptation
Resource overstretching: Attempting to manage multiple markets without systematic processes
Inconsistent branding: Different messaging and positioning across markets
Lack of market intelligence: Expanding without understanding local competition and demand patterns

AI-powered expansion solves these problems by systematically adapting successful strategies to new markets while maintaining efficiency and avoiding common pitfalls.

The Five Pillars of AI-Powered Multi-Market Scaling

1. AI Templates Balance Efficiency with Local Authenticity

The key to successful multi-market expansion is creating templates that capture your proven strategies while allowing for local market adaptation. AI can help develop these templates by analyzing what works in your successful markets and creating adaptable frameworks.

Effective scaling templates include:

Content frameworks: Proven article structures that can be adapted with local information and examples
Google Business Profile optimization: Systematic approaches to profile setup and management that work across markets
Review acquisition systems: Automated processes that adapt timing and messaging for local market preferences
Local citation strategies: Comprehensive directory and website lists that can be applied to new markets
Advertising campaign templates: Proven ad copy and targeting strategies adapted for local competition and pricing

A home services company used AI to create templates from their most successful location, then deployed them across six new markets. Each market achieved positive ROI 156% faster than their original location because they avoided the trial-and-error phase of finding what works.

2. Market-Specific Adaptation Without Losing Proven Elements

AI can analyze new target markets to identify what needs to be adapted versus what should remain consistent across all locations.

Market adaptation analysis includes:

Local competition assessment: Different competitive landscapes requiring different positioning strategies

Demographic variations: Age, income, and lifestyle differences that affect messaging and service emphasis

Seasonal pattern differences: How weather, tourism, or economic cycles vary between markets

Local terminology and preferences: Regional language differences and cultural preferences

Regulatory and licensing variations: Different requirements or restrictions across markets

A restaurant chain used AI market analysis to discover that their "comfort food" positioning worked well in suburban markets but needed to emphasize "quick healthy options" in urban business districts. This local adaptation increased new location success rates by 89%.

3. Automated Multi-Location Citation and Listing Management

Managing business listings across multiple locations manually is nearly impossible to do consistently. AI can automate citation building and monitoring across all your markets simultaneously.

Automated listing management includes:

Comprehensive directory identification: Finding all relevant local directories for each market

Consistent information deployment: Ensuring NAP (Name, Address, Phone) consistency across all platforms

Market-specific category optimization: Adjusting business categories based on local search behavior

Review platform prioritization: Focusing on the most important review sites in each market Ongoing monitoring and corrections: Maintaining accuracy as directory requirements change

A dental practice group used AI citation management to maintain consistent listings across 12 locations. When they discovered a phone number error affecting multiple locations, AI corrected it across 247 directories within 24 hours, a task that would have taken weeks manually.

4. Competitive Intelligence and Local Opportunity Identification

AI can analyze competitive landscapes in target markets before expansion, identifying opportunities and challenges specific to each location.

Market intelligence includes:

Competitor analysis: Understanding who dominates local search in each target market

Service gap identification: Finding underserved needs or market opportunities

Pricing and positioning research: How successful businesses position themselves in each market

Local partnership opportunities: Businesses and organizations that could provide referrals or collaboration

Seasonal demand patterns: Market-specific trends that affect business timing and strategy

A physical therapy clinic used AI competitive analysis to discover that their target expansion market was underserved for sports injury therapy despite having several college athletic programs. They adjusted their positioning and content strategy, capturing 34% market share within six months of opening.

5. Performance Tracking and Cross-Market Learning

AI can track performance across all markets simultaneously, identifying what works best in different locations and applying those insights to improve all locations.

Cross-market intelligence includes:

Best practice identification: Finding strategies that work exceptionally well in specific markets

Performance benchmarking: Comparing similar markets to identify improvement opportunities

Resource allocation optimization: Directing marketing spend to markets and tactics with highest ROI

Problem pattern recognition: Identifying issues that occur across multiple markets for systematic solutions Expansion prioritization: Using performance data to choose future expansion markets

The Multi-Market Scaling Process

Phase 1: Success Framework Documentation (Week 1)
Analyze and document what makes your current location successful:
- Strategy audit: Document all successful marketing tactics and systems from existing location(s)
- Performance baseline: Establish metrics that indicate success in your proven market
- Process documentation: Create step-by-step procedures for replicating successful approaches
- Content inventory: Catalog high-performing content that can be adapted for new markets
- Relationship mapping: Identify partnership and referral patterns that could be replicated

Phase 2: Target Market Analysis and Adaptation Planning (Week 2)
Research target markets to understand necessary adaptations:

- Market research: Analyze demographics, competition, and demand patterns in target markets
- Competitive landscape assessment: Understand who dominates local search and how to differentiate
- Local opportunity identification: Find underserved niches or market gaps
- Adaptation requirements: Determine what needs to change versus what should stay consistent
- Resource requirement planning: Calculate time, budget, and staff needed for each market

Phase 3: Systematic Deployment Across Markets (Week 3-4)
Launch coordinated expansion efforts using AI-powered templates:

- Citation and listing deployment: Submit to all relevant directories across all target markets
- Content adaptation and publication: Create market-specific versions of proven content
- Google Business Profile optimization: Set up and optimize profiles for each new location
- Review system implementation: Deploy automated review acquisition across all markets
- Advertising campaign launch: Start targeted campaigns adapted for each market's competition

Phase 4: Cross-Market Optimization and Learning (Ongoing)
Use performance data to improve all markets continuously:

- Performance monitoring: Track key metrics across all markets to identify patterns and opportunities
- Best practice sharing: Apply successful tactics from one market to others
- Resource reallocation: Shift marketing spend to highest-performing markets and tactics
- Expansion planning: Use success patterns to identify and prioritize future expansion opportunities
- System refinement: Improve templates and processes based on multi-market experience

Multi-Market Content Strategies

The Local Variation Approach

Create content that maintains your core messaging while incorporating local relevance:

Core framework: Proven article structure and key points that work across markets
Local examples: Market-specific case studies, customer stories, and community references
Geographic keywords: Location-specific search terms and local landmarks
Community connections: References to local events, organizations, and cultural elements
Seasonal adaptations: Different timing and emphasis based on local weather and economic patterns

The Market-Specific Deep Dive Strategy
Develop comprehensive content for each market that addresses unique local needs:
Market research content: Articles about local industry trends, regulations, or opportunities
Community involvement: Content about local events, sponsorships, and community engagement
Local problem-solving: Address challenges specific to each geographic market
Competitive differentiation: Content that positions you against local competitors
Partnership showcases: Feature local business relationships and referral sources

The Cross-Market Authority Building
Use success in one market to build credibility in others:

Case study adaptation: Success stories from established markets adapted for new markets
Expertise positioning: Use achievements from all markets to build overall authority
Multi-location social proof: Reviews and testimonials from across your market area
Regional thought leadership: Position yourself as the area expert across multiple markets
Cross-market referrals: Use satisfied customers to generate referrals in nearby markets

Scaling Strategies by Business Type

Multi-Location Service Businesses

Professional services: Emphasize consistent quality and expertise across all locations while adapting to local market needs
Home services: Focus on local response times and area-specific service challenges
Healthcare services: Address local health concerns and insurance preferences
Financial services: Adapt to local economic conditions and demographic financial needs

Franchise and Chain Businesses

Retail franchises: Balance brand consistency with local market adaptation
Restaurant chains: Maintain core menu while adapting to local tastes and preferences
Service franchises: Ensure consistent service delivery while addressing local competition
Multi-unit ownership: Optimize performance across owned units in different markets

Regional Expansion Businesses

Single-brand growth: Systematic expansion into adjacent markets using proven strategies
Market domination: Deep penetration into multiple markets within a region
Strategic acquisition: Using AI insights to identify and integrate acquired businesses
Partnership expansion: Growing through local partnerships and referral relationships

Advanced Multi-Market Techniques

The Hub and Spoke Strategy
Use your strongest market as a hub to support expansion into surrounding areas:
- Resource sharing: Centralized management and expertise deployed across markets
- Cross-market referrals: Established market customers refer to new locations
- Brand authority transfer: Success in hub market builds credibility in spoke markets
- Operational efficiency: Shared systems and processes across all markets

The Market Testing Approach
Use AI to test expansion strategies in lower-risk ways before full market entry:
- Digital-first expansion: Build online presence before physical presence
- Service area expansion: Gradually extend service areas into adjacent markets
- Partnership testing: Work with local partners before establishing direct presence
- Seasonal market entry: Test markets during peak demand periods

The Competitive Conquest Strategy
Use AI competitive intelligence to target underserved segments in established markets:
- Gap identification: Find service or geographic gaps in competitive markets
- Positioning differentiation: Enter markets with unique value propositions
- Price disruption: Use operational efficiency to compete on value
- Service innovation: Offer services or convenience competitors don't provide

Common Multi-Market Scaling Mistakes

The Cookie-Cutter Error

Using identical content and strategies without local market adaptation.

The Resource Spreading Problem
Attempting too many markets simultaneously without adequate resources for success in any.

The Consistency Neglect Issue

Allowing brand and service quality to vary significantly between markets.

The Local Intelligence Gap

Expanding without understanding local competition, regulations, or customer preferences.

The Performance Isolation Mistake
Managing each market separately instead of learning and sharing best practices across locations.

Measuring Multi-Market Success

Market-Level Performance Metrics

Revenue per market: Total business generated from each geographic area
Market penetration: Percentage of potential customers reached in each market
Customer acquisition cost by market: Efficiency of customer acquisition across markets
Market share growth: Competitive position improvement over time
Cross-Market Intelligence Metrics
Best practice transfer rate: How quickly successful strategies spread across markets
Resource allocation efficiency: ROI comparison across different markets and tactics
Brand consistency scores: Maintaining consistent customer experience across markets
Cross-market referral patterns: How customers from one market refer to others

Building Your Multi-Market Strategy

Month 1: Foundation and Planning
- Document successful strategies from established markets
- Research and analyze target expansion markets
- Develop adaptable templates and systems
- Create implementation timeline and resource allocation plan
Month 2: Initial Market Entry
- Deploy citation and listing strategies across target markets
- Launch adapted content and advertising campaigns
- Implement review and reputation management systems
- Begin local relationship building and community engagement

Month 3: Optimization and Learning
- Analyze initial performance across all markets
- Identify successful tactics and areas for improvement
- Share best practices between markets
- Adjust strategies based on local market response

Month 4+: Scaling and Expansion
- Use proven systems to enter additional markets
- Develop advanced cross-market strategies
- Build regional authority and recognition
- Plan next phase of geographic expansion

Your Multi-Market Competitive Advantage

While most businesses struggle with geographic expansion because they start over in each market, AI-powered scaling creates systematic advantages:

Accelerated market entry: Proven strategies adapted for new markets launch faster than starting from scratch

Consistent brand experience: Customers get the same quality experience regardless of location

Operational efficiency: Shared systems and processes reduce costs and management complexity

Competitive intelligence: Understanding of multiple markets provides broader strategic perspective

Risk reduction: Systematic approach reduces the typical failure rate of business expansion

Your competitors are expanding haphazardly or not at all. You're expanding systematically with AI-powered intelligence that reduces risk while accelerating success.

The businesses that master multi-market scaling don't just grow bigger, they build regional dominance that becomes INCREASINGLY ly difficult for competitors to challenge.

Key Insights

"Scaling isn't copying, it's adapting strategically."
"One proven strategy, multiple local flavors."
"AI turns expansion into regional relevance."
"Each market deserves its own story with shared success principles."
"Multiply your presence without multiplying effort through systematic intelligence."

ETHICS, TRUST, AND AUTHENTICITY IN AI-POWERED LOCAL MARKETING

Marcus runs a family law practice that had been growing steadily using AI-powered content creation and local SEO strategies. His website traffic was up 200%, his Google Business Profile was getting consistent engagement, and potential clients were finding him for all the right searches.

Then he made a mistake that nearly cost him his reputation.

In an effort to create more content faster, Marcus used an AI tool to generate a blog post about local divorce laws. He published it without careful review. The problem? The AI had generated information about a law that had been changed three months earlier, and it referenced a local courthouse procedure that hadn't been accurate in over a year.

A potential client read the article, followed the outdated advice, and had their case delayed by six weeks. When they contacted Marcus frustrated and confused, he realized his mistake. Worse, the client shared their experience in a detailed negative review that mentioned the incorrect legal information.

That experience taught Marcus a crucial lesson about AI in local business marketing: speed and efficiency are valuable, but trust and accuracy are irreplaceable.

We immediately implemented an AI ethics and quality control framework for his practice:
- Human expert review for all AI-generated content before publication
- Fact-checking protocols that verified local information and recent changes
- Clear disclosure when AI was used in content creation
- Regular content audits to catch and correct any outdated information
- Client feedback systems that caught accuracy issues quickly

Within three months, Marcus had not only recovered his reputation but strengthened it. Clients began commenting on how accurate and up-to-date his information was compared to other attorneys' websites. His review ratings improved, and referrals increased because people trusted the reliability of his content.

The lesson: AI is a powerful tool for local businesses, but it must be used responsibly with human oversight to maintain the trust that local businesses depend on.

Why Trust Matters More for Local Businesses

Local businesses operate on trust in ways that national companies don't. When you're the neighborhood dentist, the local accountant, or the contractor down the street, your reputation is everything. A single mistake or misleading piece of information can damage relationships that took years to build.

Local trust factors that AI can affect:

Accuracy of local information: Customers expect you to know current local regulations, procedures, and conditions
Personal connection: Local customers want to feel like they're dealing with someone who understands their community
Transparency: Local businesses succeed on honest, straightforward communication
Consistency: Customers expect your AI-enhanced marketing to match your actual service quality
Community responsibility: Local businesses are part of the community fabric and held to higher standards

AI can enhance these trust factors when used responsibly, or undermine them when used carelessly.

The Five Pillars of Ethical AI Marketing for Local Businesses

1. Human Oversight Ensures Local Accuracy and Authenticity

The biggest risk of AI in local marketing isn't that it sounds robotic, modern AI can write quite naturally. The risk is that it doesn't know your local community, current regulations, or recent changes that affect your customers.

Essential human oversight includes:
Local knowledge verification: Ensuring AI-generated content accurately reflects current local conditions, laws, and procedures
Community context checking: Verifying that references to local events, organizations, or cultural elements are accurate and appropriate
Service accuracy confirmation: Making sure AI descriptions of your services match what you actually provide
Seasonal relevance review: Ensuring content timing and seasonal references make sense for your local market Voice consistency maintenance: Keeping your authentic brand voice even when using AI assistance

A real estate agent discovered that AI had generated content about local school ratings using data that was two years old. In a rapidly changing market, this outdated information could have seriously misled home buyers. She implemented a review process that caught and corrected such issues before publication.

2. Transparent AI Use Builds Rather Than Erodes Trust

Some businesses try to hide their use of AI, worried that customers will think less of AI-assisted content. This approach creates risks and missed opportunities.

Transparency about AI use, when positioned correctly, can actually build trust.

Effective AI transparency includes:
Clear disclosure: Acknowledging when AI assists in content creation while emphasizing human oversight

Value explanation: Helping customers understand how AI helps you serve them better (faster responses, more comprehensive information, better availability)

Quality assurance communication: Explaining your review processes and commitment to accuracy

Human connection emphasis: Making it clear that AI enhances but doesn't replace human expertise and personal service

Mistake handling: Having protocols for quickly correcting any AI-generated errors

A veterinary clinic added a note to their AI-assisted FAQ page: "These answers combine AI research with our doctors' expertise and are reviewed by our veterinary team for accuracy. For specific medical concerns, always consult directly with our veterinarians." This transparency increased rather than decreased client confidence in the information.

3. Avoiding AI Hallucinations in Location-Specific Content

AI "hallucinations", when AI generates false information that sounds plausible, are particularly dangerous for local businesses because customers expect local expertise to be accurate.

Common AI hallucination risks for local businesses:

Outdated local regulations: AI might reference old laws, procedures, or requirements

Incorrect business hours or locations: AI might generate wrong information about local businesses or services

Non-existent local references: AI might create plausible-sounding but fake local businesses, events, or landmarks
Inaccurate statistics: AI might generate convincing but incorrect local demographic or economic data False local news or events: AI might reference local happenings that didn't actually occur

A financial advisor caught AI content that referenced a local bank branch that had closed two years earlier. Publishing that information would have sent potential clients to a non-existent location and seriously undermined credibility.

4. Maintaining Authentic Local Voice and Personal Connection

The goal of AI assistance should be to amplify your authentic voice and expertise, not replace it with generic content that could come from any business anywhere.

Preserving authenticity while using AI:

Personal story integration: Add your real experiences and client examples to AI-generated content frameworks

Local knowledge additions: Include insights that only come from actually working in your community

Brand voice consistency: Edit AI content to match your established communication style and personality

Community connection references: Add genuine local relationships and community involvement

Expert opinion injection: Include your professional insights that AI can't generate

A chiropractor used AI to create the structure for patient education articles but always added personal anecdotes from his practice and specific observations about how local lifestyle factors (like long commutes or outdoor activities) affected his patients' conditions.

5. Building Trust Through Consistent Quality and Value

AI should help you deliver more value to your local community, not just produce more content. Quality and usefulness matter more than quantity.

Quality-focused AI use includes:

Value-first content creation: Using AI to research and structure content that genuinely helps your local customers

Accuracy verification processes: Systematic checking of AI-generated information before publication

Regular content updates: Using AI to help maintain current, relevant information

Customer feedback integration: Using AI to analyze and respond to customer questions and concerns

Service improvement focus: Using AI insights to actually improve your service delivery, not just your marketing

Ethical AI Implementation Guidelines

Content Creation Ethics

Always verify local facts: Check any AI-generated information about local laws, procedures, events, or businesses Maintain professional standards: Ensure AI-assisted content meets the same quality standards as your professionally created content

Respect competitor fairness: Use AI for your own improvement, not to unfairly attack or undermine local competitors

Honor client confidentiality: Never use AI tools that might compromise client privacy or confidential information

Provide genuine value: Focus on creating content that actually helps your local community, not just improves your search rankings

Customer Interaction Ethics

Honest capability representation: Don't oversell what AI can do or present AI responses as human expertise

Privacy protection: Ensure any AI tools you use protect customer data appropriately

Response accuracy: Take responsibility for AI-generated responses and correct any mistakes quickly

Personal touch maintenance: Balance AI efficiency with genuine human connection

Cultural sensitivity: Review AI content to ensure it's appropriate for your local community's values and culture

Business Practice Ethics

Fair competition: Use AI to compete through better service and value, not deceptive practices
Truth in advertising: Ensure AI-assisted marketing claims are accurate and supportable
Community responsibility: Consider how your AI use affects your role in the local business community
Employee consideration: Be transparent with staff about AI use and how it affects their roles
Long-term thinking: Consider how AI practices affect your long-term reputation and community relationships

Building an Ethical AI Framework for Your Business

Step 1: Establish AI Use Policies

Create clear guidelines for how AI can and cannot be used in your business:
- Acceptable AI applications: Content research, first drafts, data analysis, routine task automation
- Required human oversight: Local information verification, professional advice, customer service quality control
- Prohibited uses: Replacing professional expertise, generating content without review, compromising client confidentiality
- Quality standards: All AI-assisted content must meet the same standards as human-created content
- Transparency requirements: When and how to disclose AI assistance to customers

Step 2: Implement Review Processes

Develop systematic approaches to ensure AI-generated content maintains quality and accuracy:
- Fact-checking protocols: Verify local information, statistics, and references
- Voice consistency reviews: Ensure content matches your authentic brand voice
- Professional standards checking: Confirm content meets industry and legal requirements
- Customer perspective evaluation: Review content from the customer's point of view
- Regular audit schedules: Systematically review AI-assisted content for ongoing accuracy

Step 3: Train Your Team

Ensure everyone who uses AI in your business understands ethical guidelines:
- AI capability education: Help staff understand what AI does well and where it needs human oversight
- Quality standards training: Teach team members to maintain professional

standards with AI assistance

- Ethics awareness: Discuss the importance of honesty, accuracy, and community responsibility
- Review process training: Ensure everyone knows how to properly check and improve AI-generated content
- Customer communication: Train staff to appropriately discuss AI use with customers when relevant

Step 4: Monitor and Improve

Continuously evaluate and improve your ethical AI practices:

- Performance tracking: Monitor how AI use affects customer satisfaction and business results
- Mistake learning: When errors occur, update processes to prevent similar issues
- Community feedback: Pay attention to how your AI use is perceived in your local community
- Industry standards: Stay current with developing best practices for AI in your industry
- Regular policy updates: Adjust your AI guidelines as technology and standards evolve

Common Ethical Pitfalls and How to Avoid Them

The "Set It and Forget It" Trap

Problem: Publishing AI-generated content without ongoing review and updates
Solution: Regular content audits and update schedules

The Over-Automation Risk

Problem: Using AI for tasks that require human judgment or local expertise
Solution: Clear boundaries on where AI helps versus where humans must lead

The Generic Content Problem

Problem: AI-generated content that doesn't reflect your unique local knowledge and perspective
Solution: Always add personal insights and local expertise to AI-generated frameworks

The Accuracy Assumption Error

Problem: Assuming AI-generated information is correct without verification
Solution: Systematic fact-checking processes, especially for local and professional information

The Transparency Avoidance Mistake
Problem: Hiding AI use in ways that could damage trust if discovered
Solution: Appropriate disclosure that positions AI as a tool that helps you serve customers better

Industry-Specific Ethical Considerations

Professional Services (Legal, Medical, Financial)
- Regulatory compliance: Ensure AI-assisted content meets professional licensing and ethical requirements
- Disclaimer protocols: Clear statements about when professional consultation is needed
- Confidentiality protection: Never use AI tools that might compromise client privacy
- Accuracy standards: Higher verification requirements for professional advice content

Service-Based Businesses (Contractors, Repair, Personal Services)
- Service representation accuracy: Ensure AI descriptions match actual capabilities and service quality
- Local knowledge verification: Confirm information about local codes, permits, and procedures
- Safety information accuracy: Double-check any AI-generated safety or technical information
- Customer expectation management: Make sure AI-enhanced marketing reflects actual service delivery

Retail and Hospitality
- Product information accuracy: Verify AI-generated product descriptions and availability information
- Local community sensitivity: Ensure AI content respects local culture and values
- Customer service consistency: Balance AI efficiency with personal service expectations
- Promotional accuracy: Confirm AI-assisted offers and promotions are valid and legal

Building Long-Term Trust Through Responsible AI Use

The businesses that will thrive with AI are those that use it to become better at serving their local communities, not just better at marketing to them.

Responsible AI use creates trust by:

Improving service quality: Using AI insights to better understand and serve customer needs
INCREASINGLY accessibility: Making your expertise and services more accessible through AI-enhanced communication
Enhancing consistency: Providing reliable, accurate information across all customer touchpoints
Demonstrating transparency: Being honest about how you use technology to serve customers better
Maintaining human connection: Using AI to enhance rather than replace personal relationships

Your Ethical AI Competitive Advantage

While some businesses rush to use AI without considering ethical implications, those that implement responsible AI practices build sustainable competitive advantages:

Enhanced reputation: Community recognition for reliable, trustworthy business practices
Customer loyalty: Deeper relationships built on consistent quality and transparency
Risk reduction: Fewer mistakes and problems that could damage your business
Team confidence: Staff who understand and support how AI enhances their work
Long-term sustainability: Practices that will remain valuable as AI technology continues evolving

Your competitors might use AI carelessly, creating short-term gains but long-term risks. You can use AI responsibly to build lasting competitive advantages based on trust, quality, and community connection.

The local businesses that master ethical AI use don't just get better marketing results, they become more trustworthy, reliable partners in their communities. That trust becomes a competitive moat that's extremely difficult for competitors to cross.

Key Insights

"AI is a powerful tool, but your judgment and integrity guide its use."
"Never let automation create distance between you and your customers."
"Local trust is built on local accuracy, verify everything."
"AI can write fast, but humans keep it real and reliable."
"Ethics isn't optional, it's the foundation of sustainable success."

THE FUTURE: LOCAL BUSINESS MEETS AI INNOVATION

Amy owns a boutique fitness studio that had mastered everything we'd covered in the previous chapters. Her AI-powered local SEO was driving consistent leads, her review management system was building strong reputation, and her voice search optimization was capturing mobile customers perfectly.

But Amy was thinking beyond current AI applications. She wanted to understand what was coming next and how to prepare her business for the future of AI and local search.

That's when I introduced her to some emerging AI technologies that are about to transform how local businesses connect with customers.

We started with a pilot program that gave Amy a glimpse of the future:

Predictive customer intent: AI that analyzed local search patterns and weather forecasts to predict when people would be most likely to search for fitness classes, allowing Amy to adjust her advertising and class schedules proactively
Conversational search optimization: Content specifically designed for AI chatbots and virtual assistants that could recommend her studio when people asked questions like "where can I find a beginner-friendly yoga class that's not intimidating?"
Visual search integration: Optimization that helped people find her studio when they took photos of her building or used image search to find "studios like this one"
Hyper-local personalization: AI that could tailor her website content and recommendations based on exactly where in her service area someone was searching from
Community prediction modeling: AI analysis of local demographic shifts, development patterns, and lifestyle trends to predict where demand for fitness services would grow

The results were impressive. Amy's lead quality improved 67% because AI was connecting her with customers at the perfect moment of intent. Her customer lifetime value increased 34% through better matching of services to customer needs. Most importantly, she was building competitive advantages that would be extremely difficult for other studios to replicate.

But the real value wasn't just better current performance, it was positioning Amy's business to thrive as AI continues transforming how people find and choose local businesses.

Why the Future of Local Search Is More Personal and Predictive

The current wave of AI in local marketing is just the beginning. The next generation of AI applications will make local search more conversational, predictive, and personalized than most business owners can currently imagine.

Key trends shaping the future:
Conversational AI everywhere: Voice assistants, chatbots, and AI search engines will handle INCREASINGLY ly complex local business queries
Predictive customer matching: AI that knows when customers will need services before they search
Visual and multimodal search: Customers finding businesses through photos, videos, and mixed-media searches
Hyper-local personalization: AI that tailors recommendations based on exact location, time, and personal preferences
Integrated ecosystem experiences: Seamless connection between search, navigation, payment, and service delivery

The businesses that understand and prepare for these changes will have enormous advantages over those that wait until these technologies are widespread.

The Five Pillars of Future-Ready Local AI Strategy

1. Conversational AI Integration Across All Customer Touchpoints
The future of local search isn't about optimizing for keywords, it's about optimizing for conversations. Customers will INCREASINGLY ly ask AI assistants complex questions and expect nuanced, helpful responses.

Next-generation conversational optimization includes:
Complex query handling: Preparing for questions like "I need a family-friendly restaurant with outdoor seating, good vegetarian options, and parking, somewhere between my office and my kid's soccer practice"
Context-aware responses: AI that understands follow-up questions and maintains conversation context
Appointment scheduling integration: Conversational AI that can check availability and book services during the search process
Multi-step problem solving: AI assistants that can handle complex service requests requiring multiple interactions
Emotional intelligence: AI that can recognize customer urgency, frustration, or specific needs and respond appropriately.

A dental practice is already testing conversational AI that can handle complex scheduling requests like "I need a cleaning appointment next week sometime after 2 PM, but not on Wednesday, and I need to know if my insurance covers it first." The system can check schedules, verify insurance, and book appointments without human intervention.

2. Predictive Local Demand and Customer Behavior Analysis

AI is becoming sophisticated enough to predict when customers will need services before they actively search, creating opportunities for proactive customer engagement.

Predictive AI applications include:

Seasonal demand forecasting: AI that predicts service demand based on weather patterns, local events, and historical data

Life event prediction: Identifying customers who are likely to need specific services based on demographic and behavioral patterns

Maintenance schedule prediction: For service businesses, AI that can predict when customers will need routine service

Economic trend analysis: Understanding how local economic conditions will affect demand for different services

Competitive opportunity prediction: Identifying when competitors might be vulnerable or when market opportunities will emerge

A landscaping company uses predictive AI to identify homeowners who are likely to need spring cleanup services based on their property type, previous service history, and local weather patterns. They reach out proactively and capture business before competitors even know demand is developing.

3. Visual and Multimodal Search Optimization

The future of local search won't be limited to text and voice. Visual search, augmented reality, and mixed-media searches will create new ways for customers to find local businesses.

Visual search preparation includes:

Image optimization: Ensuring your business photos are optimized for AI image recognition and visual search

Augmented reality readiness: Preparing for customers who will point their phones at your location to get instant information

Video search optimization: Creating video content that AI can analyze and recommend in video search results

Product and service visual recognition: Helping AI understand what you offer through visual content

Location-based visual cues: Optimizing for customers who search by showing photos of nearby landmarks or areas

A restaurant is preparing for visual search by ensuring their food photos are optimized with detailed alt text and schema markup that helps AI understand exactly what dishes they serve. They're also preparing for AR applications where customers could point their phone at the restaurant and see reviews, menu items, and availability instantly.

4. Hyper-Personalized Local Experiences at Scale

AI will enable unprecedented personalization of local business experiences, tailoring recommendations and content to individual customers' exact situations and preferences.

Hyper-personalization includes:

Location-context personalization: Different experiences based on exactly where customers are when they search

Time-sensitive customization: Recommendations that change based on time of day, day of week, and seasonal factors

Behavioral preference learning: AI that remembers and adapts to individual customer preferences over time

Service matching: Connecting customers with the exact services and staff members that best match their needs

Dynamic pricing and offers: Personalized promotions based on customer value and situation

A professional services firm is testing AI that can personalize their website content based on whether someone is searching during business hours (showing immediate consultation availability) or after hours (emphasizing email contact and scheduling), and whether they're searching from a business district (B2B focus) or residential area (personal services focus).

5. Integrated Local Ecosystem Participation

The future of local business AI won't be about individual tools, it will be about participating in integrated ecosystems where search, navigation, payment, review, and service delivery work together seamlessly.

Ecosystem integration includes:

Smart city integration: Participating in city-wide digital infrastructure and services

Transportation integration: Connecting with navigation apps, ride-sharing, and public transportation

Payment ecosystem participation: Seamless payment integration across all customer touchpoints

Cross-business collaboration: AI-enabled partnerships and referrals with complementary local businesses

Community platform integration: Participating in local digital communities and neighborhood apps

A group of local businesses is pilot-testing an AI ecosystem where customers can search for "date night downtown," get restaurant recommendations, make reservations, get navigation directions, pay for parking, and receive follow-up service all through connected AI systems.

Preparing Your Business for the AI-Driven Future

Building Future-Ready Infrastructure

Data collection and organization: Systematically collecting customer data that will enable future AI applications

API-ready systems: Ensuring your business systems can integrate with future AI platforms and services

Mobile-first optimization: Preparing for AI applications that will primarily happen on mobile devices

Voice-optimized content: Creating content structures that work well with current and future voice AI

Visual content library: Building high-quality visual assets optimized for AI recognition and recommendation

Developing AI-Enhanced Customer Experiences

Conversational customer service: Testing AI chatbots and virtual assistants for customer interaction

Predictive service delivery: Using AI to anticipate customer needs and provide proactive service

Personalized communication: Implementing AI that can customize messaging for different customer segments

Automated relationship management: AI
 systems that help maintain and strengthen customer relationships over time Cross-channel experience consistency: Ensuring AI enhancements work seamlessly across all customer touchpoints

Building Competitive AI Advantages

Early adoption of emerging technologies: Testing new AI applications before competitors understand their value

Data advantage development: Collecting and organizing data that gives you superior AI training opportunities

Partnership strategy: Building relationships with AI technology providers and other forward-thinking businesses

Team AI literacy: Training your staff to work effectively with AI tools and understand their implications

Innovation culture: Creating organizational openness to AI experimentation and continuous improvement

Industry-Specific Future Scenarios

Healthcare and Professional Services

AI diagnostic assistance: AI that can help customers understand symptoms and know when to seek professional help

Predictive health services: Identifying customers who might benefit from preventive or routine services

Regulatory AI compliance: AI systems that help maintain compliance with changing regulations

Telemedicine integration: Seamless connection between local practice and AI-enabled remote services

Retail and Hospitality

Inventory prediction AI: Anticipating customer demand for specific products or services

Dynamic experience customization: Real-time adjustment of service delivery based on customer preferences

Event-driven marketing: AI that can capitalize on local events and opportunities instantly

Customer journey optimization: AI that improves every step of the customer experience

Service-Based Businesses

Predictive maintenance: AI that can predict when customers will need service before problems occur

Resource optimization: AI that helps optimize scheduling, routing, and resource allocation

Quality prediction: AI that can predict and prevent service quality issues before they affect customers

Market expansion AI: Using AI to identify and evaluate new market opportunities

Potential Risks and How to Prepare

Technology Dependence Risks

Over-automation concerns: Ensuring AI enhances rather than replaces human connection

System failure preparation: Having backup plans when AI systems experience problems

Skills gap management: Maintaining human capabilities even as AI handles more tasks

Cost escalation planning: Preparing for INCREASINGLY costs of advanced AI applications

Competition and Market Changes

AI arms race dynamics: Staying competitive as AI becomes table stakes for local businesses

Big tech platform dependence: Reducing vulnerability to changes in major AI platforms

Market disruption preparation: Anticipating how AI might change customer behavior and expectations

Regulatory change adaptation: Preparing for new regulations around AI use in business

Customer Trust and Privacy

Data privacy management: Ensuring customer data is protected as AI applications become more sophisticated

Transparency maintenance: Keeping customers informed about AI use without overwhelming them

Human connection preservation: Using AI to enhance rather than replace personal relationships

Quality assurance scaling: Maintaining service quality as AI handles more customer interactions

Building Your Future-Ready Strategy

Phase 1: Foundation Assessment and Planning (Month 1)
Evaluate your readiness for advanced AI applications:

- Current AI audit: Assess how well your current AI implementations are performing
- Data infrastructure review: Determine what data you're collecting and how it could enable future AI
- Technology stack evaluation: Review whether your current systems can integrate with advanced AI
- Team capability assessment: Evaluate your team's AI literacy and training needs
- Competitive landscape analysis: Understand how competitors are preparing for AI evolution

Phase 2: Advanced AI Experimentation (Months 2-3)
Begin testing next-generation AI applications:

- Conversational AI pilots: Test advanced chatbots and voice assistants for customer service
- Predictive analytics implementation: Begin using AI to predict customer behavior and demand
- Visual search optimization: Prepare your visual content for image and AR search
- Personalization testing: Experiment with AI-driven content and experience personalization
- Ecosystem integration exploration: Identify opportunities to participate in AI-enabled business ecosystems

Phase 3: Integration and Optimization (Months 4-6)
Scale successful AI applications and integrate them into your operations:

- Successful pilot scaling: Expand AI applications that show clear business value
- System integration: Connect AI tools with your existing business systems
- Team training advancement: Develop deeper AI capabilities within your organization
- Customer experience enhancement: Use AI insights to improve overall service delivery
- Performance measurement: Establish metrics for evaluating advanced AI effectiveness

Phase 4: Innovation and Leadership (Months 6+)
Become a leader in AI-enhanced local business:

- Industry thought leadership: Share insights and best practices with other local businesses
- Advanced application development: Create custom AI solutions for your specific business needs
- Partnership development: Build relationships with AI technology providers

and innovative local businesses
- Market expansion: Use AI advantages to expand into new markets or services
- Future preparation: Stay ahead of the next wave of AI innovations

Your AI-Powered Future Advantage

The local businesses that prepare for the AI-driven future now will have enormous advantages over those that wait:

First-mover benefits: Early access to AI capabilities before they become widespread

Data advantages: Better data collection and organization enabling superior AI applications Customer relationship depth: Using AI to build stronger, more personalized customer connections

Operational efficiency: AI-enhanced operations that provide cost advantages and service quality improvements

Innovation reputation: Recognition as a forward-thinking business that customers and partners prefer

Your competitors are still catching up to current AI applications. You can be preparing for the next generation.

They're reacting to AI changes. You can be anticipating and preparing for them.

They're using AI as a tool. You can build AI into the foundation of how you serve customers and compete.

The Long-Term Vision

The future of local business isn't about replacing human connection with artificial intelligence. It's about using AI to enable deeper, more meaningful, more valuable relationships with your local community.

AI will help you:
- Understand customer needs before they express them
- Deliver personalized experiences that feel genuinely caring
- Anticipate and solve problems before they become frustrations
- Connect customers with exactly the right services at the right time
- Build community relationships that transcend individual transactions

The local businesses that master this integration of AI capability with human authenticity won't just survive the AI revolution, they'll lead it.

They'll become the businesses that other local companies study and emulate. They'll attract the best customers, the most talented employees, and the strongest community support.

Most importantly, they'll demonstrate that the future of AI in local business isn't about choosing between technology and humanity, it's about using technology to become more human, more connected, and more valuable to the communities they serve.

The future is coming whether you prepare for it or not. The question is: will you shape it, or will it shape you?

Key Insights

"Search is becoming anticipation, AI helps you meet customers before they know they're looking."

"The future isn't just digital, it's physical experiences enhanced by AI intelligence."

"Prediction is the new optimization, know what customers need before they ask."

"AI will understand context, location, and timing, position yourself to be the answer."

"Lead locally today by building the AI-enhanced tomorrow your community needs."

LEADING LOCAL WITH AI, AND HEART

When I started helping local businesses transform their digital presence over a decade ago, the challenge was simple: get found online. A well-designed website, some basic SEO, and a Google Business Profile could make the difference between thriving and struggling.

Today, that's just table stakes.

The local businesses succeeding now, and positioning themselves for the future, aren't just using AI tools randomly. They're integrating AI strategically into every aspect of how they connect with, serve, and grow their local customer base.

But here's what I've learned after working with hundreds of local businesses: the most successful AI implementations don't replace the human elements that make local businesses special. They amplify them.

The Complete AI-Powered Local Business System

Throughout this book, we've built a comprehensive system that transforms how local businesses approach digital marketing:

Foundation (Chapters 1-2): Using AI to audit your current performance and discover the keywords your customers actually use when they need what you provide

Content and Presence (Chapters 3-4): Creating locally relevant content at scale and optimizing your Google Business Profile to capture customers at the moment of decision

Reputation and Authority (Chapters 5-6): Building systematic review acquisition and earning local links that establish your business as a trusted community resource

Advanced Optimization (Chapters 7-8): Capturing voice search traffic and measuring what actually drives business growth, not just website visits

Strategic Integration (Chapters 9-10): Coordinating paid and organic efforts for maximum impact and scaling successful strategies across multiple markets

Sustainable Success (Chapters 11-12): Maintaining trust and authenticity while preparing for the next generation of AI-enhanced local marketing

Each element builds on the others, creating a system that's more powerful than any individual tactic.

What Makes This Different

This isn't just another book about digital marketing tactics. It's a guide to building sustainable competitive advantages using AI in ways that strengthen rather than weaken your connection to your local community.

It's systematic, not random: Every strategy connects to others in a coordinated approach that compounds results over time

It's local-first, not generic: Every technique is specifically designed for businesses that serve geographic markets and depend on local relationships

It's human-centered, not technology-obsessed: AI amplifies your expertise and authenticity instead of replacing them

It's results-focused, not activity-focused: Every chapter emphasizes outcomes that drive actual business growth

It's future-ready, not just current: The strategies position you for the next wave of AI developments while delivering immediate results

The Businesses That Will Dominate Local Markets

After working with hundreds of local businesses implementing these strategies, I can predict with confidence which ones will dominate their markets in the years ahead:

They use AI to understand their customers better: They know exactly what their ideal customers search for, when they search, and what converts browsers into buyers

They deliver consistent value at scale: They provide helpful, accurate, locally relevant information across all digital touchpoints

They build trust systematically: They earn reviews, create content, and manage their online reputation with AI-enhanced processes that maintain authentic voice and local expertise

They integrate rather than isolate: They coordinate all their marketing efforts, paid ads, SEO, social media, email, using AI insights to maximize combined impact

They prepare for the future while excelling in the present: They're building capabilities and collecting data that will enable next-generation AI applications

Most importantly, they use AI to become better local businesses, not just better marketers.

Your Next Steps: From Reading to Results

Reading about AI strategies won't transform your business. Implementing them systematically will.

Here's how to turn what you've learned into measurable results:

Month 1: Foundation and Quick Wins

- Complete an AI-powered audit of your current local search presence (Chapter 1)
- Research and document the conversational keywords your customers actually use (Chapter 2)
- Optimize your Google Business Profile with AI-suggested improvements (Chapter 4)
- Implement automated review requests for satisfied customers (Chapter 5)

Months 2-3: Content and Authority Building

- Create a geo-targeted content calendar using AI research (Chapter 3)
- Launch systematic local citation building and link acquisition (Chapter 6)
- Optimize your website for voice search queries (Chapter 7)
- Set up AI-powered analytics that connect marketing activities to business results (Chapter 8)

Months 4-6: Integration and Scaling

- Coordinate your paid advertising with organic content strategy (Chapter 9)
- Document successful strategies for potential geographic expansion (Chapter 10)
- Implement ethical AI guidelines and quality control processes (Chapter 11)
- Begin experimenting with next-generation AI applications (Chapter 12)

Months 6+: Leadership and Innovation

- Refine and scale tactics that deliver the best ROI
- Share insights with other local business owners and establish thought leadership
- Explore advanced AI applications specific to your industry
- Build partnerships with other forward-thinking local businesses

The Compound Effect of AI-Enhanced Local Marketing

The real power of these strategies isn't in any individual tactic, it's in how they work together to create compound advantages over time.

When your AI-optimized Google Business Profile showcases content that targets voice search queries discovered through AI keyword research, supported by reviews acquired through intelligent automation, and reinforced by locally relevant links earned through systematic outreach, you create a competitive position that's extremely difficult for competitors to replicate.

Each element makes the others more effective:
- Better content attracts more quality links
- More quality links improve search rankings for your content
- Better search visibility generates more review opportunities
- More reviews increase click-through rates from search results
- Higher click-through rates signal quality to search algorithms

This compound effect means businesses that implement AI systematically don't just get incrementally better results, they often see exponential improvements in lead quality, conversion rates, and customer lifetime value.

The Human Element: Why AI Makes Local Businesses More Personal, Not Less

The biggest misconception about AI in local business is that it makes marketing more robotic and impersonal. In my experience, the opposite is true when AI is implemented thoughtfully.

AI handles the repetitive, time-consuming tasks that prevent local business owners from focusing on what they do best: serving customers and building community relationships.

Instead of spending hours managing citations: You focus on delivering exceptional service that earns organic word-of-mouth referrals

Instead of manually tracking competitor activities: You concentrate on innovating and improving your own service delivery

Instead of guessing about customer needs: You use AI insights to anticipate and solve problems proactively

Instead of creating generic content: You add personal insights and local expertise to AI-generated frameworks

Instead of reactive customer service: You build predictive systems that address customer needs before they become problems

The local businesses that master AI don't become less human, they become more capable of expressing their humanity at scale.

Your Competitive Advantage Starts Now

While most local businesses are still deciding whether to embrace AI, you have the opportunity to build advantages that will compound for years.

Your competitors are using AI randomly, if at all. You can implement it systematically.

They're treating AI as a cost center. You can make it a profit center.

They're worried about AI replacing human connection. You can use it to strengthen community relationships.

They're reacting to changes in local search. You can anticipate and prepare for them.

The businesses that act on these strategies in the next 90 days will have significant advantages over those that wait until AI becomes "mainstream" in local marketing.

A Personal Note: Why This Matters Beyond Business

I've spent over a decade helping local businesses succeed online because I believe strong local businesses create strong communities. When the neighborhood restaurant, the family dentist, and the local service provider thrive, everyone benefits.

AI gives local businesses tools that were previously available only to large corporations. For the first time, a single-location business can compete with regional chains on sophistication while maintaining the personal touch that makes local businesses special.

This isn't just about better marketing, it's about economic opportunity, community resilience, and the future of local entrepreneurship.

When you use AI to build a stronger local business, you're not just growing revenue. You're creating jobs, supporting families, and contributing to a thriving local economy.

The Choice Is Yours

You have a choice: lead or follow.

You can implement these AI strategies now and build sustainable competitive advantages, or you can wait until your competitors force you to catch up.

You can use AI to strengthen your connection to your local community, or you can let others use it to capture the customers you should be serving.

You can be part of the solution that helps local businesses thrive in an AI-enhanced world, or you can be disrupted by businesses that understand these opportunities better.

The tools are available. The strategies are proven. The only question is whether you'll use them.

The Future of Local Business Is Bright

Despite concerns about AI replacing human workers or making business impersonal, I'm optimistic about the future of local business.

AI will make it easier for local businesses to:
- Understand and serve their customers better
- Compete with larger companies on capability while maintaining personal

touch
- Build sustainable competitive advantages based on local expertise and community connection
- Anticipate and adapt to changing customer needs and market conditions

The local businesses that embrace AI thoughtfully won't just survive, they'll become the beating heart of thriving communities.

They'll be the businesses that residents recommend proudly, that visitors remember fondly, and that other entrepreneurs study and emulate.

Your AI-Enhanced Local Business Awaits

The strategies in this book work. They've worked for hundreds of businesses across dozens of industries in markets large and small.

They'll work for your business too, if you implement them.

The question isn't whether AI will transform local business. It already is.

The question is whether you'll be among the businesses leading that transformation or struggling to catch up.

Your customers are already using AI to find local businesses. They're speaking to voice assistants, asking complex questions, and expecting personalized, immediate responses.

The businesses that understand and prepare for this AI-enhanced future will capture those customers. The ones that don't will wonder why their phones stopped ringing.

The choice is yours. The time is now.

Your AI-enhanced local business, and the thriving community it serves, is waiting for you to take the first step.
Start today. Your future customers are already searching.

Key Insights

"AI shouldn't distract local businesses, it should multiply their reach."
"Visibility without context is just noise, AI gives your business context."
"You can't scale trust, but you can automate the signals that build it."
"People don't search, they ask. AI helps you answer."
"Local means personal. AI helps you do that personally, at scale."

The future of local business is AI-enhanced, community-connected, and more human than ever.

ABOUT THE AUTHOR

Phil Tucker is a digital marketing strategist who has spent over a decade helping local service businesses transform their online presence into predictable lead-generation engines.

As the founder of Be Famous Media, established in 2012, Phil has worked with hundreds local businesses across dozens of industries, from single-location family practices to multi-market service companies. His signature "Results Drive System ™" has helped businesses consistently double and triple their qualified leads through data-driven local marketing strategies.

Phil's expertise lies in translating complex digital marketing concepts into practical, implementable strategies that work for real business owners with real budgets and real time constraints. He specializes in businesses that serve specific geographic markets: home services contractors, healthcare practices, professional services, restaurants, retail stores, and other community-focused businesses.

What sets Phil apart:

- Results-focused approach: Every strategy is tested with actual businesses and measured by revenue impact, not vanity metrics
- Local market expertise: Deep understanding of how geographic businesses build trust and compete in their communities
- Systematic methodology: Creates repeatable processes that businesses can implement without technical expertise or large marketing teams
- Authentic voice: Maintains the conversational, knowledgeable-friend approach that makes complex marketing concepts accessible

Phil's AI integration journey began in 2022 when he recognized that artificial intelligence wasn't just changing how people searched, it was transforming how local businesses could understand, reach, and serve their customers. Rather than jumping on AI trends randomly, he spent months systematically testing AI applications with his client base, documenting what worked and what didn't.

The strategies in "INCREASINGLY Local" come directly from this hands-on experience implementing AI tools with real local businesses facing real competitive challenges.

Before founding Be Famous Media, Phil developed his understanding of local markets and community-focused business through various marketing roles, always gravitating toward businesses that serve their neighbors rather than anonymous online audiences.

When he's not helping local businesses dominate their markets, Phil can be found exploring new AI applications, analyzing local search trends, and figuring out how emerging technologies can help small businesses compete with larger corporations without losing their authentic community connections.

Phil believes the future of local business isn't about choosing between high-tech efficiency and authentic relationships, it's about using technology to build stronger, more personal connections with the communities that local businesses serve. His mission is simple: help local businesses use AI strategically to become the companies their communities choose first, competitors respect, and neighbors recommend proudly.

CLIENT CASE STUDIES

Client Privacy Notice: The following case studies are based on real client results and genuine implementations of AI-powered local marketing strategies. To protect client privacy, names, locations, and identifying details have been changed. All performance metrics represent actual achieved outcomes.

Case Study 1: Sarah's Physical Therapy Practice
Industry: Healthcare/Physical Therapy
Business Size: 2-6 therapists
Timeline: 6 months
Location: Mid-sized metropolitan area
The Challenge
Sarah owned a well-established physical therapy practice that was generating 10-15 new patient inquiries per month through her website. While her clinical reputation was excellent, she struggled to differentiate herself in a competitive market with several larger therapy chains.
Initial Situation:
- 10-15 monthly inquiries from website
- Generic website content that could apply to any practice
- Limited online visibility for specific conditions
- Competition from larger chain practices with bigger marketing budgets

The AI Strategy Implementation
Voice Search Optimization: Created content targeting conversational searches like "physical therapy for back pain after car accident" and "sports injury rehab near me"
Hyper-Local Content: Developed neighborhood-specific content addressing local demographics and activities (office workers with desk-related issues, weekend warriors with sports injuries)
AI-Powered Patient Journey Mapping: Used AI to analyze patient inquiry patterns and optimize content for different stages of the decision process
Predictive Content: Created condition-specific content based on seasonal injury patterns and local activity trends
The Results
6-Month Outcomes:
- 40+ qualified inquiries monthly (167% increase)
- Practice expansion: Grew from 2 therapists to 6
- Second location opening: Demand justified geographical expansion
- Improved patient quality: Higher show-up rates and treatment completion

Key Success Factors:
- Content matched actual patient language and concerns
- Local relevance increased trust and credibility
- Predictive approach captured patients before competition
- Systematic implementation maintained consistent growth

Implementation Details
Month 1-2: Content audit and voice search optimization Month 3-4: Hyper-local content development and publishing Month 5-6: Advanced AI analytics and predictive content creation

Tools Used: AI keyword research platforms, voice search optimization tools, predictive analytics software

---

Case Study 2: Jessica's Lawn Care Service

Industry: Home Services/Landscaping

Business Size: Owner + 2-3 seasonal employees

Timeline: 2 months

Location: Suburban residential area

The Challenge

Jessica had built a successful lawn care business through referrals and door-to-door marketing, but online visibility was poor. She was competing for broad terms like "lawn care services" against national companies with large marketing budgets.

Initial Situation:

- Decent website traffic but low conversion rates
- Competing for generic, high-competition keywords
- Phone calls were inconsistent and seasonal
- Difficulty differentiating from larger competitors

The AI Strategy Implementation

Conversational Keyword Discovery: AI analysis revealed customers searched for specific needs like "who can cut my grass tomorrow" and "lawn service that does edging too"

Hyper-Local Content: Created content for specific neighborhoods and local landmarks

Intent-Based Optimization: Focused on high-intent searches indicating immediate need

Service-Specific Targeting: Developed content around specific services rather than generic lawn care

The Results

2-Month Outcomes:

- 156% increase in qualified leads
- 73% higher conversion rate from conversational keywords vs. generic terms
- Consistent phone calls throughout the season
- Premium pricing acceptance due to specific service positioning

Key Success Factors:

- Discovered low-competition, high-intent keywords
- Content matched how customers actually think and speak
- Local specificity built trust and relevance
- Quick implementation showed fast results

Implementation Details

Week 1-2: AI keyword research and content strategy development Week 3-6: Content creation and website optimization Week 7-8: Performance analysis and refinement

Most Effective Keywords:

- "who can cut my grass tomorrow"
- "lawn service that does edging too"
- "grass cutting near [local elementary school]"
- "emergency lawn care after storm damage"

Case Study 3: David's Multi-Location Therapy Practice
Industry: Mental Health/Counseling
Business Size: 5 locations, 12+ therapists
Timeline: 3 months
Location: Large metropolitan area (multiple neighborhoods)

The Challenge

David's practice served five different neighborhoods, each with distinct demographics and needs. His marketing approach was generic across all locations, missing opportunities to connect with specific community concerns.

Initial Situation:

- Generic content that didn't address neighborhood-specific needs
- Low conversion rates despite decent traffic
- Inconsistent performance across different locations
- Difficulty capturing diverse demographic segments

The AI Strategy Implementation

Geographic Content Personalization: Created neighborhood-specific content addressing local demographics and concerns

AI Demographic Analysis: Used AI to understand different community needs and mental health challenges

Location-Specific SEO: Optimized each location for hyper-local searches

Cultural Sensitivity Optimization: Tailored messaging for diverse community preferences

The Results

3-Month Outcomes:

- 89% increase in website traffic
- 214% increase in consultation requests
- Dramatically improved lead quality - better client-therapist matches
- Reduced no-show rates due to better initial matching

Key Success Factors:

- Hyper-local content resonated with specific communities
- AI demographic analysis revealed hidden opportunities
- Location-specific optimization captured neighborhood searches
- Improved matching led to better client outcomes

Content Examples

Riverside Neighborhood: "Supporting Working Parents in Riverside: Managing Stress When School Schedules Change"

Downtown Area: "Mental Health Resources Near Downtown Metro Station: Evening Appointments Available"

Tech District: "Coping with Job Market Changes: Career Counseling for Tech Workers"

Case Study 4: Mike's Plumbing Company
Industry: Home Services/Plumbing
Business Size: Owner + 2 plumbers
Timeline: 6 weeks
Location: Mid-sized city

The Challenge

Mike thought his plumbing business was performing well online with a professional website and Google Business Profile. However, he had no systematic understanding of what was actually driving business results.

Initial Situation:
- Business information inconsistent across 47 online directories
- Phone number listed 3 different ways across platforms
- Two duplicate Google Business Profiles splitting reviews
- 8.2-second website load time on mobile
- No clear understanding of lead sources

The AI Strategy Implementation

Comprehensive AI Audit: Used AI tools to identify technical and citation issues across hundreds of platforms

Citation Consistency: Systematically corrected business information across all directories

Technical Optimization: Fixed mobile performance and user experience issues

Duplicate Listing Resolution: Consolidated Google Business Profiles and redirected review authority

The Results

6-Week Outcomes:
- 340% increase in local search visibility
- Significant increase in phone calls (hired another plumber)
- Improved professional appearance online
- Better customer experience through faster, mobile-friendly website

Specific Issues Resolved:
- 31 specific technical and citation problems identified by AI
- Business name inconsistent across 23 directories
- Address format variations (Street vs. St.)
- Phone number in 3 different formats
- Critical mobile usability problems

Implementation Timeline

Week 1: AI audit and problem identification Week 2-3: Technical fixes and citation corrections Week 4-5: Google Business Profile consolidation Week 6: Performance monitoring and final optimizations

Case Study 5: Kevin's Bakery
Industry: Food Service/Retail
Business Size: Family-owned bakery
Timeline: 90 days
Location: Downtown area

The Challenge

Kevin's bakery had been successful with traditional local search optimization, ranking well for searches like "bakery downtown" and "fresh bread delivery." However, website traffic was plateauing despite growing mobile search trends.

Initial Situation:

- Good rankings for traditional text searches
- Plateauing website traffic despite market growth
- Missing voice search traffic opportunities
- Content optimized for typing, not speaking

The AI Strategy Implementation

Voice Search Analysis: Discovered customers ask complete questions like "Where can I get gluten-free muffins for my daughter's school party tomorrow?"

Conversational Content: Created FAQ sections answering complete customer questions

Mobile Experience Optimization: Improved mobile site performance for voice search users

Local Context Integration: Added location-specific information for voice assistant compatibility

The Results

90-Day Outcomes:

- 127% increase in mobile traffic
- Improved inquiry quality - customers with specific, immediate needs
- Voice search visibility for conversational queries
- Higher conversion rates from voice-initiated traffic

Voice Search Examples Captured:

- "Where can I get birthday cake today"
- "Best croissants near me right now"
- "Bakery open early Sunday morning"
- "Gluten-free options downtown bakery"

Key Learnings

- Voice searches are longer and more conversational
- Mobile users have immediate intent and higher conversion rates
- Local context is crucial for voice assistant recommendations
- FAQ format works well for voice search optimization

Case Study 6: Tom's Auto Repair Shop
Industry: Automotive Services
Business Size: 3-person shop
Timeline: 4 months
Location: Suburban area
The Challenge
Tom consistently delivered excellent automotive service and had loyal customers, but his online presence was nearly invisible. He had only 23 reviews scattered across platforms over three years, while competitors had hundreds.
Initial Situation:
- 23 total reviews across all platforms (3 years)
- Invisible in local search results
- Excellent service quality but poor online reputation
- Main competitor had 847 reviews despite lower quality work
- "Good work should speak for itself" mentality

The AI Strategy Implementation
Automated Review Timing: AI-powered system identified optimal moments when customers were happiest (after successful repairs, quick turnarounds)
Smart Customer Segmentation: Directed happy customers to public reviews, concerned customers to private feedback
Response Automation: AI-assisted responses maintaining Tom's authentic voice
Multi-Platform Strategy: Systematic approach across Google, Yelp, and Facebook
The Results
4-Month Outcomes:
- Review count: From 23 to 312 reviews
- Search ranking improvement: From page 2 to top 3 positions
- 156% increase in phone calls
- 34% revenue growth from increased online visibility

Quality Improvements:
- Reviews became more detailed and specific
- Customers mentioned specific services and experiences
- Higher average rating due to systematic approach
- Reduced impact of occasional negative reviews

Implementation Details
Month 1: System setup and customer journey analysis Month 2-3: Automated review requests and response management Month 4: Performance optimization and scaling
Key Success Factors:
- Timing requests when customers were most satisfied
- Making review process easy and convenient
- Maintaining authentic voice in all communications
- Systematic approach vs. random asking

Case Study 7: James's Roofing Company
Industry: Home Services/Roofing
Business Size: 8-12 employees
Timeline: 6 months
Location: Regional service area

The Challenge

James had implemented various AI marketing strategies but couldn't connect marketing activities to actual business results. He knew he was getting calls but didn't understand which efforts were driving the most valuable customers.

Initial Situation:
- Multiple marketing activities running simultaneously
- No clear attribution of leads to specific channels
- Couldn't identify highest-value customer sources
- Generic analytics showing traffic but not business impact

The AI Strategy Implementation

AI-Powered Analytics Dashboard: Integrated system showing complete customer journey from search to signed contract

Geographic Performance Analysis: Neighborhood-level insight into customer value and marketing effectiveness

Predictive Demand Forecasting: AI analysis of weather patterns and storm damage predictions

Customer Value Attribution: Tracking which marketing activities generated highest-value projects

The Results

6-Month Outcomes:
- 156% revenue increase through better focus on effective activities
- 340% higher conversion rate from storm-damage-related searches vs. generic roofing terms
- 67% higher average project value from certain neighborhoods
- Predictive advantage: Could prepare for demand spikes 2-3 days before storms

Key Insights Discovered:
- Storm damage searches converted 340% better than generic terms
- Certain neighborhoods had 67% higher average project values
- Weather patterns predicted demand spikes with 2-3 day lead time
- Emergency services had highest profit margins but required different marketing approach

Advanced Analytics Applications

Neighborhood Analysis: Identified high-value service areas for focused marketing
Seasonal Optimization: Predicted busy periods for crew and inventory planning
Competitive Intelligence: Tracked competitor activities and market share changes
Customer Lifetime Value: Focused marketing on customer segments with highest long-term value

Case Study 8: Carlos's Auto Repair Expansion
Industry: Automotive Services
Business Size: Single location expanding to 4 locations
Timeline: 8 months
Location: Multi-city expansion
The Challenge
Carlos had built a successful auto repair business that dominated local search in his original city. He wanted to expand to three neighboring cities without starting from scratch in each new market.
Initial Situation:
- Successful single-location business
- Wanted to expand to 3 additional cities (30-45 minutes away)
- Traditional expansion would require years and high costs
- Risk of diluting original location success

The AI Strategy Implementation
Success Pattern Analysis: AI documented what made original location successful for replication
Market Intelligence: AI analysis of competition and opportunities in target markets
Template Scaling: Adaptable frameworks for content, citations, and reputation management
Cross-Market Learning: AI identified successful tactics to apply across all locations
The Results
8-Month Outcomes:
- Successfully established presence in all 3 target markets
- $180,000 additional annual revenue from new locations
- 67% faster profitability in new markets vs. original location timeline
- Original location continued growing while expanding

Key Success Factors:
- Systematic replication of proven strategies
- Market-specific adaptation without starting from zero
- Automated citation and reputation management across locations
- Cross-location learning and optimization

Expansion Timeline
Months 1-2: Success documentation and target market analysis Months 3-5: Systematic launch in first expansion market Months 6-8: Simultaneous launch in markets 2 and 3 Month 8+: Cross-market optimization and refinement
Lessons for Multi-Market Expansion:
- Success patterns can be documented and replicated
- AI automation makes multi-location management feasible
- Market-specific adaptation is crucial for local relevance
- Systematic approach reduces risk and accelerates growth

Case Study 9: Lisa's Physical Therapy Paid/Organic Integration
Industry: Healthcare/Physical Therapy
Business Size: 3-location practice
Timeline: 4 months
Location: Metropolitan area

The Challenge

Lisa had been running Google Ads and SEO as separate strategies managed by different people. Her cost per acquisition was INCREASINGLY while organic progress felt slow, creating budget pressure and internal conflict.

Initial Situation:

- Google Ads and SEO managed separately with different goals
- Rising cost per acquisition in paid advertising
- Slow organic progress with unclear ROI
- No coordination between paid and organic messaging
- Budget competition between channels

The AI Strategy Implementation

Integrated Keyword Strategy: Used paid conversion data to prioritize organic content creation

Message Coordination: Aligned ad copy with website content for consistent user experience

Cross-Channel Attribution: AI tracking of complete customer journey across touchpoints

Budget Optimization: Dynamic allocation based on combined channel performance

The Results

4-Month Outcomes:

- 43% decrease in overall cost per acquisition
- 127% increase in organic traffic by targeting proven converting keywords
- 89% increase in total leads while maintaining flat marketing costs
- Improved lead quality through consistent messaging

Integration Benefits:

- Paid data informed organic strategy priorities
- Organic content supported paid ad messaging
- Combined approach dominated more search results
- Budget efficiency improved through coordinated efforts

Implementation Strategy

Month 1: Analysis of existing paid/organic performance and integration opportunities Month 2: Coordinated content creation and message alignment Month 3: Cross-channel tracking and attribution implementation
Month 4: Optimization based on integrated performance data

Case Study 10: Marcus's Law Practice Ethics Recovery
Industry: Legal Services/Family Law
Business Size: Solo practitioner
Timeline: 3 months recovery
Location: Mid-sized city
The Challenge
Marcus had been successfully using AI for content creation when he published a blog post with outdated legal information. A potential client followed the incorrect advice, experienced case delays, and left a detailed negative review about the misinformation.
Initial Situation:

- 200% increase in website traffic from AI content
- Consistent Google Business Profile engagement
- One major accuracy mistake with public consequences
- Reputation damage from detailed negative review
- Loss of trust in AI-assisted content creation

The Recovery Strategy Implementation
Ethical AI Framework: Implemented human expert review for all AI-generated content
Fact-Checking Protocols: Systematic verification of local laws and procedures
Transparency Policy: Clear disclosure of AI assistance with human oversight
Quality Control: Regular content audits and client feedback systems
The Results
3-Month Recovery Outcomes:

- Full reputation recovery within 3 months
- Stronger reputation than before - clients commented on accuracy and reliability
- Improved review ratings due to increased attention to quality
- Increased referrals based on reliability reputation

Lessons Learned:

- AI requires human oversight, especially for professional advice
- Transparency about AI use can build rather than hurt trust
- Quality control systems prevent larger reputation issues
- Recovery is possible through systematic approach to accuracy

Ethical AI Implementation
Content Review Process: Every AI-generated piece reviewed by legal expert Local Law Verification: All legal information checked against current regulations Client Feedback System: Regular accuracy checks through client interactions Transparency Statements: Clear disclosure of AI assistance and human oversight

119

Cross-Case Study Analysis

Common Success Factors
1. Systematic Implementation: All successful cases followed structured approaches rather than random AI experiments
2. Local Relevance: Hyper-local content and community connection were crucial across industries
3. Human Oversight: AI amplified human expertise rather than replacing it
4. Performance Measurement: Clear metrics and continuous optimization drove sustained results
5. Authentic Voice: Maintaining business personality while using AI tools

Industry-Specific Insights

Healthcare/Professional Services: Trust and accuracy are paramount; transparency builds credibility Home Services: Immediate need searches and emergency optimization drive highest value Food/Retail: Voice search and mobile optimization crucial for location-based businesses Multi-Location: Systematic scaling with local adaptation prevents starting from scratch

Timeline Patterns

Quick Wins (2-6 weeks): Technical fixes, citation cleanup, basic optimization

Medium-term Growth (2-4 months): Content strategy results, reputation building

Long-term Advantages (6+ months): Market dominance, systematic scaling, competitive moats

Investment vs. Return

Lower Investment, High Return: Citation cleanup, voice search optimization, review systems
Medium Investment, Sustained Return: Content strategy, integrated marketing, analytics
Higher Investment, Transformational Return: Multi-market expansion, advanced AI integration

These case studies demonstrate that AI-powered local marketing success comes from systematic implementation, maintaining authenticity, and focusing on customer needs rather than just technology capabilities.